The Story
of Delamere House
and Delamere Park

The Story
of Delamere House
and Delamere Park

A.D.Coxhead & R.M.Bevan

C.C.Publishing
(Chester)

First published in 2008 by
C.C. Publishing, Chester (UK), CH3 7RX
Tel: 01829 741651.

British Library cataloguing in Publication Data.
A catalogue record for this book is available from the
British Library.

ISBN   978-0-949001-37-5

Origination by C.C.Publishing (Chester).

www.cc-publishing.co.uk

Contents

Foreword

As head of the Wilbraham family I have been asked to write a Foreword to this incredible book on Delamere House and Delamere Park. It is full of interesting stories about the life that was lived in the years gone by.

The tale goes from the building of Delamere Lodge, in the 18th century, the demolition of Delamere House, occupation by the American army during the Second World War, the Polish/Eastern European camp and on to the current Delamere Park development of outstanding quality homes. The information and pictures etc that have been discovered and reproduced give a fascinating insight into life of the past centuries.

This book will stand as a fine example of Wilbraham history and the family's devotion to the County of Cheshire.

Hugh D.Wilbraham

Acknowledgments

The authors wish to acknowledge and thank a number of individuals who have provided invaluable assistance on the long journey to completion of "The Story of Delamere House and Delamere Park". The first of these is Hugh Wilbraham without whose co-operation and unflinching support this book simply could not have been compiled. Hugh has been an immense source of information throughout and the Wilbraham family photographs which he has provided are a delight.

Particular appreciation is also due to Andrew Pozniak, Joe Janik and Halina Jaworowski who were children of the Delamere Camp Polish community. Their photographs, memories and contacts helped to unlock the most difficult area of research, since there appears hardly a reference in the public archives appertaining to the life and times of the Polish and Eastern European communities during the twenty years following the Second World War. Hopefully, this book helps, in a small way, to put the record straight.

Others who have notably assisted include: Jennifer Austin, Clive & Elizabeth Brown, John Dolman, David & Edith Fraser, the late Gordon Fergusson, Elizabeth Johnson, Richard Morris, Norman Shelley, Barbara Smith, Dorothy Taylor, Gareth & Averil Thomas, Stan Urbanski, David & Jane Wheeldon, Tom Wright.

The authors also acknowledge the support provided by Cheshire Libraries and the Cheshire Record Office, and English Heritage who have supplied the high resolution aerial photographs showing the various phases of the old camp.

Finally, a general heartfelt thanks to all who have contributed information and memories.

Introduction

There are so many facets to "The Story of Delamere House and Delamere Park" that the title hardly does justice to the subject. We could have added "Early Cuddington", "The Wilbrahams", "The Camp", "The Americans", "The Poles", because, in a sense, this is an account spanning an entire millennium and beyond, a microcosm of English history.

The old village of Cuddington, once set within the ancient forest of Delamere, has been shaped and chiselled by the melting ice-caps, the Norman lords and the medieval settlers, but more than anything, it is what it is because of the arrival, in the 18th century, of the Wilbrahams of Nantwich, a family rooted in Cheshire antiquity.

The first of the Wilbrahams here erected a fashionable hunting lodge which later generations transformed into a Victorian mansion, Delamere House, standing at the centre of a great estate, thousands of acres stretching from Cuddington and Crowton to the Staffordshire borders. The Wilbrahams developed the farms, built the cottages and promoted a rural vibrancy that now dims into the distant past, recalled only in the pages of books as such as this.

The changing fortunes of the 20th century redefined the landscape and, like the other great estate owners, the Wilbrahams found their idyllic world crumbling around them, so that by the time of the Second World War, though the cottages and the farms survived, Delamere House was no more. Only the once majestic English parkland remained and soon it was to be occupied by others, from all walks of life, all creeds and nationalities, transported from opposite sides of the globe. Young Americans came in their thousands to join the fight to save the free world and when the tyranny of Hitler had been eradicated, those who had suffered the most appalling misery, the Polish people and other Eastern Europeans, found refuge on Wilbraham land.

Almost twenty years they stayed and when the last were integrated into the wider Mid Cheshire community, the developers moved in, to create Delamere Park, a concept born of a dream.

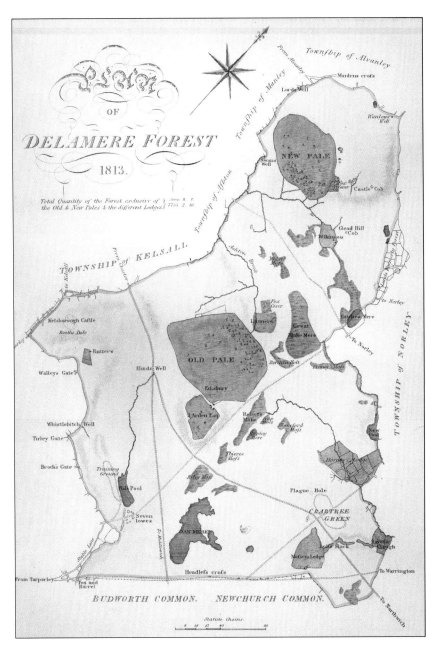

Delamere Forest 1813 at the time of an Act of Parliament to enclose 7,755 acres of wastes and commons. Approximately half of the pink area was retained by the Crown with the remainder principally allotted to existing large landowners. The Delamere Forest wastes and commons of Cuddington, Crowton, Norley and Kingsley had already been enclosed during the 18th century.

x

Early Cuddington

DELAMERE PARK sits atop the highest ground on the Cuddington plateau, rich agricultural land formed millions of years ago in the wake of the final ice cap as it receded north-westward, leaving behind the sands of Cheshire and the Kingsley-Cuddington ridge. On the crown of the steep-sided Cuddington plateau, created by the meltwater gouging the valleys of Cuddington Brook and Small Brook, remained a saucer-shaped aquifer and above it, over millennia, evolved fertile ground, well-watered and ripe for settlement (1).

Water is in abundance, especially where the aquifer's springline overflows north down the hollow of Cuddington Lane, into a sluice near to Cuddington Hall Farm. At one time there was a well here, opposite to the driveway to the farm, and the water is sufficiently close to the surface to keep full an old horse trough, in Cuddington Lane. Indeed, the digging of a relatively shallow hole hereabouts is guaranteed to strike water and well sites are recorded at Delamere Lodge and also near to the Gardener's Cottage, in Woods Lane.

On the park itself, in the vicinity of Foxes Hey, the Wilbraham family created an ornamental lake, out of a large, natural pond, and the contractors, whilst carrying out excavations during the building of the housing estate, encountered flooding in the general vicinity of Ravensfield and a

The Delamere Horn carried by the Master Forester as a symbol of his power.

11

These egg-shaped, split granite cobbles often turn up in the gardens and the fields around the edge of Delamere Park. They were left by the receding glaciers in a layer of boulder clay till overlying deep iceberg-filled sand. The 50p coin indicates their size.

"massive release of water" near to where The Burrows is now located.

This plentiful supply of water and the fertile land has supported a settlement here since pre-historic times. The high ground afforded a commanding position, undoubtedly the best in the area to defend, other than the Old Pale, and when the Romans invaded Britain, circa AD40, a sizeable clearing for rudimentary agriculture had already been carved out of the birch, alder and heathland of the ancient forest. And as several military roads passed nearby, these Cuddington clearing dwellers might have been close enough, but fortunately far enough away, to look down upon the comings and goings of the Romans who ruthlessly destroyed any settlement within "four bow shots", a fate that befell the Iron Age encampment of Eddisbury. The principal Roman road was North Watling Street, from Chester to York (more or less along the line of today's A556 through Sandiway), and from it, at Crabtree Green, a spur ran towards the present day White Barn railway bridge. Here it merged with a road from Whitchurch which, from a vantage point close by the present railway station, then aligned north-east to Weaverham and a crossing of the River Weaver.

The name "Cuddington" is Viking, "Sandiway" Old English, and the first records appear in the 7th century when the Archbishop of Canterbury established the Parish of Weaverham. Sandiway was a mere hamlet, a lordship within Weaverham parish, whereas Cuddington, sometimes referred to in later documents as "Cuddington-cum-Bryn", was of considerably greater importance, being one of seven townships, including Crowton, Onston and parts of Norley, held by the Saxon, Earl Edwin.

For three centuries dwellers on the Cuddington ridge lived relatively untroubled until the Norman invasion (1066) and the brutal reaction by William the Conqueror to uprisings in the North. With its handful of wooden, straw-thatched cottages, Cuddington was "laid waste" like so many other Cheshire villages, including Weaverham where only the wrecked Saxon stone church remained standing. As part of this purge across the North, almost all the original landowners vanished, either put to death, or reduced to the status of villeins or serfs on their own land.

Cheshire was designated a County Palatine and the first Norman Earl of Chester, Hugh of Avaranches (Hugh Lupus), was granted enormous power and privilege. Cuddington is not mentioned in the Domesday Book (1086), but then only nine churches and nineteen mills were recorded in the entire county, along with thirty-one Norman-held manors, including Weaverham. The ancient forest, "Mara", to the west, and "Mondrem", to the east, was defined as a royal hunting forest and cruel laws were rigorously enforced. Foresters were appointed, their rule absolute within the King's land, and Cuddington, severed from Norman Weaverham, fell directly under this harsh regime. The Crown's representative in the forest, and holding almost exclusive powers over life and death,

Weaverham Parish Church, early 20th century. Cuddington was one of seven townships within Weaverham parish held by the Saxons.

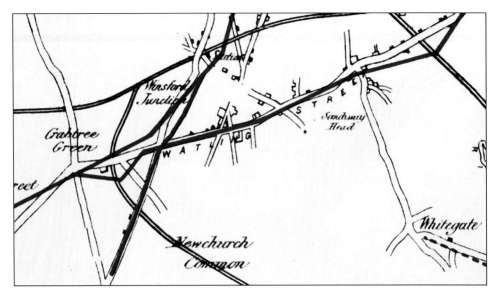

Approximate alignments of Roman roads in the district, from a plan produced in the late 19th century. North Watling Street passed through Sandiway (A556) with a spur at Crabtree Green to link with the Whitchurch–Warrington road (A49). Early settlers high on the Cuddington plateau would have had a clear view of the marching Roman legions.

was the Master Forester and Chief Bowbearer, the first of whom was Ranulph de Kingsley who was granted, by the 3rd Earl of Chester in 1123, the "Manor Seigniory and Fee of Kingsley" (2). Through marriage and inheritance, a share in the Fee of Kingsley and the office of Master Forester passed into the Done family, initially of Crowton Hall and later of Utkinton Hall. The Dones held the title and the quarter share in the Fee of Kingsley for over four-hundred years until they descended to the Crewe and then the Arderne families.

It is significant to the story of Delamere Park that Cuddington remained King's land until the middle of the 18th century, whereas Weaverham became part of the estates endowed, in 1277, by King Edward I when he founded Vale Royal (Whitegate), the greatest and largest Cistercian abbey in his kingdom. The western boundary of the abbey domains was designated as "Peytefinstey", a long-established Saxon trackway that was effectively the demarkation line between the forests of Mara and Mondrem. Historians have suggested that Peytefinstey aligned with the Roman road from Whitchurch, but this is largely incorrect. Research has shown that Peytefinstey followed the line of the present Kennel Lane and Weaverham Road before passing through Gorstage to Weaverham Church. On the east side of Peytefinstey was Sandiway, being part of Weaverham and the Vale Royal Abbey domains, whilst to the west was Bryn Common, Cuddington and the King's land. At the founding of the abbey, "Codynton" is referred to as "villae infra forestam de Mara et Mondrem".

Elsewhere, the precise boundaries of old Cuddington are difficult to establish but, as far as Delamere Park is concerned, they may reasonably be deduced from the topography, early maps and an extremely important 17th century legal parchment, discovered amongst early Wilbraham documents held at the Cheshire Record Office. The maps indicate tenements around the area of Top Farm, Poplar Farm and Cuddington Bank, to the east of what has been variously named over the centuries as Riddings Lane, Town Lane, Park Lane and Cuddington Lane, and this, with its vantage point and proximity to water, was the centre of the ancient settlement of Cuddington.

GRANT by John Done of Cuddington, yeoman, and William Done, his son and heir, to Thomas Gill of Cuddington, yeoman; reciting that WHEREAS the sd. Thomas Gill has late purchased from Gilbert Ireland of Hutt (Co. Lancs), Esq. several parcels of land in CUDDINGTON called the Roughhay and the Broomfeilds from which there has usually been a cartway and bridleway through certain parcels of land calle John Dones two pittfall Riddings in CUDDINGTON aforesaid and so through the common lane to Croton Hall, and WHEREAS the sd. Thomas Gill before the sealing of these presents ha renounced and disclaimed the sd. bridleway to the sd. John Done and William Done, NOW the sd. John Done and William Done grant to the said Thomas Gill --- one cartway and bridleway for all manner of carriages of the breadth of 4 yards in and through a parcel of land called the towne-feild through the lane at the lower end being South East from the said parcel called the Roughhaye through the sd. Townfeild lane so far as the said John and William claim t be their land towards the town lane of CUDDINGTON, and another cartway or bridleway from the brink of Richard You ditch through the sd. parcel called the townefeild through the lane by the South West side thereof from the sd. parcel of land called the Broomfoilds through the sd. Townfeilds lane as far as the sd. John Done and William Done claim to be their land towards the town lane of Cuddington.

A typed copy of the revealing 1660 Done parchment.

Life would have been good for tenement farmers on the fertile land of the Cuddington plateau with its ancient Bryn Mill, in Pinfold Hollows. There has probably been a mill here for a thousand years, although the Domesday Book lists only nineteen for the entire county of Cheshire.

The parchment relates to the granting of a cartway and a bridleway, by "John Done of Cuddington, yeoman, and William Done, his son and heir", and indicates, at this time (May 1660), a long-established lane crossing through the centre of the Delamere Park site, from Riddings Head (the "Wilbraham Gate") towards Bag Lane and its junction with Bent Lane. The parchment appears to extinguish this lane in favour of an alternative across Done land. The line of the present-day public footpath from Poplar Cottages, in Cuddington Lane, was the preferred route, this being "Townfields Lane" which passed by, or crossed, the "Townfield" at which point it turned sharply to the north, to emerge on Bag Lane below The Riddings.

This document is unambiguous in stating that the alternative route passed "... as far as the sd. John Done and William Done claim to be their land towards the town lane of Cuddington". In other words, proof positive that the site of Delamere Park was Done land.

A member of Master Forester Done lineage, John Done, as stated in the parchment, was a "yeoman", a man holding a small estate. His name also appears on the 1664 Hearth Tax Roll for Cuddington when he held two hearths, marking him as one of the most important householders in the township and, given the parchment description, it is extremely likely he was living on the site of Delamere Park, i.e. the most fertile piece of ground in the district.

The oldest detailed map of the village is the Tithe Map of 1839, sixty years after the Wilbrahams moved to the village, but all is not as it seems. Computer enhancement shows this was probably overlaid on an earlier map, pre-dating the Wilbrahams. On the site of Delamere Park is an area marked as "Old House Meadow", and with it an eccentric-shaped enclosure, approximately one-hundred yards across, located precisely in front of the mound now known as the "Captain's Tree". There is also a clearly defined access to this enclosure from Norley Road, more or less at the present day Delamere Park Way West entrance onto the park.

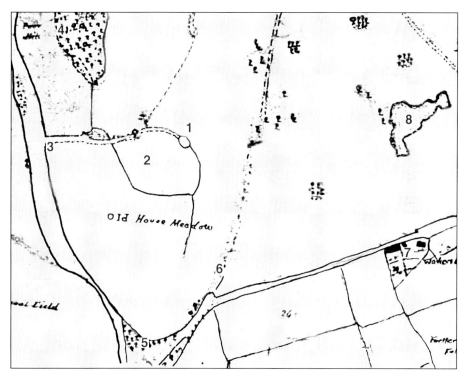

A section of the 1839 Tithe Map showing "Old House Meadow" marked with: 1.The mound upon which the Captain's Tree stands; 2. Eccentric-shaped enclosure in front of the mound; 3. Entrance to the enclosure, what is now the Delamere Park Way West junction; 4. Poor Hill; 5. Riddings Head, where the Wilbraham Gate is now sited; 6. The original driveway to Delamere Lodge; 7. Two of the Cuddington tenements/crofts on Riddings Lane/Town Lane; 8. Ornamental pond created by the Wilbrahams.

The enclosure, the access and the map term "Old House Meadow", clearly point to the existence of an early dwelling here, probably Yeoman John Done's house, evidence of which may have been unearthed by Elizabeth Johnson, of Ravensfield, when she undertook a Millennium "Time Team" dig in her rear garden, near to the "Captain's Tree". Elizabeth Johnson carefully excavated a metre cube of ground and her finds turned up twenty-seven hand-made, square-headed nails and a number of fragments of floor tile. Intriguingly, the Cheshire archaeological department thought the nails had survived from the burning of a 17th, or 18th, century cart, or thickset door, whilst the tiles were, possibly, of medieval origin.

Together, all these factors strongly suggest that although the Wilbrahams have been connected with Delamere Park for centuries, they were certainly not the first occupiers.

The Captain's Tree, a Cedar of Lebanon, planted to commemorate the birth of George Hugh de Vernon Wilbraham, in 1890. The mound has existed here for centuries.

The Wilbrahams
of Nantwich

THE first record of the Wilbrahams, or Wilburghams, appears in Cheshire as early as 1174 with the birth of Richard de Wilburgham whose son, also Richard, (born circa 1204) married Margery, or Maud, de Vernon, the eldest daughter and co-heiress of Warin de Vernon, the powerful Lord of Shipbrook (now part of Northwich). Shipbrook was one of fifteen Cheshire manors granted at the time of the Norman conquest to Margery's paternal ancestor, William, Lord of Vernon, in Normandy.

The Wilbraham Coat of Arms.

The Wilbrahams, on the other hand, probably had Anglo-Saxon roots connected with the settlement of Wilbraham, in Cambridgeshire, noted as "Wilburgeham" in the Anglo-Saxon Chronicles, circa 1,000. James Hall, in his authoritative "History of Nantwich", has the family in Cambridgeshire during the reign of Henry II (1133-1189) and there is a later link, albeit a tenuous one, through Sir Roger Trumpyngton, of Trumpington (near to Wilbraham, Cambridgeshire) who also married a daughter of the Vernons of Cheshire.

To further confuse the origins of the Wilbrahams, one also has to consider the name "Wildebor" which occurs in many early records relating to the Nantwich area, notably within 276 Wilbraham family papers acquired in 1959/60 by the Cheshire Record Office. One document, for example, refers to a marriage settlement, in 1300, of Cecily, "daughter of Aytrop de Mulynton, to

19

Randle, son of William Wildebor". Perhaps it was all down to medieval spelling and the Wildebors evolving into the Wilburghams/Wilbrahams.

How it all came about is not important to this account and it would certainly have been of little consequence to Richard de Wilburgham and Margery de Vernon whose union produced at least three daughters, the eldest of whom carried part of the Barony of Shipbrook into her marriage with Robert de Winnington. Meanwhile, upon the death of Margery de Vernon, Richard de Wilburgham married Letitia Venables, the daughter and coheiress of Sir William Venables whose ancestor, Gilbert Venables, huntsman to the Dukes of Normandy, had been granted the Barony of Kinderton (Middlewich). Through this second marriage, Richard de Wilburgham settled in the manor of Radnor, Congleton, became Lord of the Manor of Warmingham and, knighted, held the office of Sheriff of Cheshire, circa 1259. It is worthy of note here that the two marriages of Richard de Wilburgham created an anomaly over later usage of the Christian name "Vernon" within the Wilbraham family (e.g. George Hugh de Vernon Wilbraham, 1890-1962) as, in fact, the lineage descends from the Venables, and not the Vernons.

Richard de Wilburgham and Letitia Venables' son and heir was William de Wilburgham from whom the line descended to Thomas de Wilbraham who, in 1401-02, married Margaret Golborne, daughter and heiress of John Golborne, Lord of Woodhey, near to Nantwich. Upon the death of his father-in-law, Thomas de Wilbraham assumed the Woodhey title and so began Nantwich's great Wilbraham dynasty.

The Wilbrahams of Delamere Lodge/House, Cuddington (subsequently the senior line) were descended from Thomas and Margaret's second son, Ranulph (or Randle) Wilbraham, whilst other principal Nantwich branches later included the "Wilbrahams of Dorfold", the "Wilbrahams of Reaseheath" and the "Wilbrahams of Rode", the latter descending to such aristocratic lines as Lord Skelmersdale, the Earl of Derby, Lord Egerton of Tatton, and Lord Alvanley. The "Wilbrahams of Woodhey" line became extinct in 1692 and afterwards the Woodhey estates passed through marriage to the Tollemaches of Helmingham and later Peckforton Castle.

In 1570 Richard Wilbraham, grandson of Randle Wilbraham, the founding father of the "Delamere" line, is recorded as residing in Nantwich town, at Sweetbriar Hall, in Hospital Street, a property erected by the family a century earlier. From Sweetbriar Hall, Richard Wilbraham commissioned the building of a new family seat, Townsend House, in Welsh Row, and he also commenced the Wilbraham Diary, a remarkable family journal to which, for the past four-hundred years, most successive heads of the family have contributed.

Richard Wilbraham, of Townsend House, owned several thousand acres of land, principally in South Cheshire, and was the proprietor of "twelve salthouses, with ninety-six leads (pans)", in Nantwich. He had three brothers, one of whom was Sir Roger Wilbraham (1533-1616), Solicitor General for Ireland and, later, Master of Requests to the Royal Court. In 1602, Sir Roger purchased the Dorfold Hall estate, located on the outskirts of Nantwich, the title to which he passed to his youngest brother, Ralph Wilbraham. At Dorfold Hall a section of panelling still exists depicting the armorial shields and crest of the Delamere Master Forester, Sir John Done, who, in 1598, married Dorothy Wilbraham, the daughter of Sir Thomas Wilbraham, of Woodhey.

Richard Wilbraham, the builder of Townsend House, died in 1612 and was succeeded by his grandson, Thomas Wilbraham who had been born and raised in the highest of London society, a connection that was possibly the reason why, in August 1617, King James I, whilst on a tour of the North, chose to stay overnight at Townsend House. Rather surprisingly, since he had provided excellent hospitality to the royal party, Thomas was not included amongst over one hundred knights dubbed by the king during his journey. The explanation, handed down through the generations, is that, on the morning of the royal party's departure, Thomas had to attend important legal business in Chester and was, therefore, unable to escort the king to the Staffordshire border, hence the award of a knighthood, either by accident or by design, was bestowed upon Thomas's replacement escort. Thomas wrote in the Wilbraham Diary:

> Uppon the 25th of August 1617 King James at his returne forth of Scotland came to this Towne of Nantwich and lay one night at my house, at the same tyme there were with him the Duke of Lenox, Ld

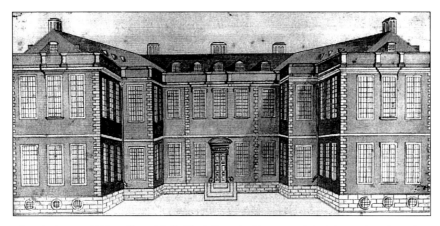

South front of Woodhey Hall, Faddiley, built around 1690 on the site of an earlier hall where the founder of the Townsend House/Delamere family line, Ranulph (or Randle) Wilbraham, spent his formative years. Woodhey Hall was demolished circa 1740 and all that remains is the family chapel which is maintained by the Woodhey Chapel Trust.

Still surviving in Hospital Street, Nantwich, is Sweetbriar Hall, an early home of the Wilbrahams, built during 15th century. It was one of the few buildings to escape the Great Fire of Nantwich, in 1583.

Founded in 1705 by Roger Wilbraham, the Widows' Almshouses in Nantwich.

Steward of the King's household, the Duke of Buckingham, Master of the Horse, the Earle of Pembrooke, Ld Chamberlaine of the King's household, and divers others Lords and Knights. Upon the 26th day he went to the Church where Doctor Dod preached before him, who shortly after was sworne his Chaplaine. At his returne from Church he went to the Brynepitt and after dinner went to Bromley to my Ld Gerard's house.

Later, as an eminent barrister, Thomas Wilbraham spent much of his time in London though, perhaps because of the looming conflict, he was living in Nantwich when Civil War erupted in Cheshire and he was made a prisoner in his own Townsend House for refusing to lend money to the Parliamentarian cause. A petition organised by influential townspeople helped to exonerate him and, set at liberty, he retired to Sussex where he died in 1643.

The great conflict between Parliament and Sovereign plunged all into turmoil and the Wilbraham fortune was not revived until after the Restoration when, incidentally, Thomas's son, Roger Wilbraham, was nominated as one of

Welsh Row, the medieval drovers' road for Welshmen taking cattle into Nantwich to exchange for salt. The horse and trap is passing Townsend House. In 1780 George Wilbraham provided land here, behind the black and white cottages, to erect York Buildings where Nantwich's cloth fairs were held. Nantwich Police Station and Courts were later built on the site of Townsend House garden.

an intended new order of knighthood, styled "Knights of the Royal Oak"; unfortunately, like his father, Roger missed out on a knighthood as the institution was never carried into effect. Roger was High Sheriff of Cheshire in 1669-70, the first native Nantwich townsman to hold the position, and a marble monument was erected to his memory in the parish church.

In 1664, Roger's family estate was valued at £1,000 per annum and this was further increased four years later through purchase, from the Stanleys, of Weaver Hall, with over 1,000 acres of land alongside the River Weaver, south of Winsford. A long association with the Weaver Navigation also commenced at this time and came to be a highly profitable, long-term venture when Roger's son, Randle Wilbraham, was named as one of five Cheshire gentlemen granted

Townsend House, in a ruinous condition by the mid-18th century, is described in George Ormerod's "History of Cheshire", as "having been lofty and spacious, with large bay windows surrounded by numerous out-buildings of timber and plaster, the gardens having high brick walls, stone ornaments of armorial bearings and grotesque devices". Richard Wilbraham moved into the completed house in August 1580, the first of six generations to live here. In 1818, the house was converted into the Townsend Brewery. and demolished in 1964. Sold in 1990 the site is now occupied by the King's Court residential development.

the right, by Act of Parliament in 1721, to develop the river in order to service the burgeoning Northwich and Winsford salt industry. The Wilbrahams were involved in the Weaver Navigation for over two-hundred years until nationalisation after the Second World War.

Throughout their time in the Nantwich district, members of the Wilbraham family were great benefactors and guardians of the rights and interests of local people. For example, in 1558, the Wilbrahams of Woodhey possibly set up the first school in Cheshire when they bequeathed £6-13s-4d annually for the monks of Combermere Abbey to educate local children at Acton, provided, in keeping with the family's tradition of piety, they prayed daily for Wilbraham souls! As to the Wilbrahams of Townsend: they built and endowed almshouses in Nantwich, supported initiatives to assist the poor and, as late as 1860, a century after moving from the town, provided a good deal of the finance required to build Nantwich Grammar School, in Welsh Row.

Following Randle Wilbraham's death, in 1732, his son Roger resided only occasionally at what had become a rather dilapidated Townsend House and he settled in Bridge Street, Chester upon marriage to Elizabeth Brooke, the daughter of Sir Thomas Brooke, of Norton. Seven years later Elizabeth died in childbirth having already had five children, none of whom survived her. Roger was not long a grieving widower and, in 1740, at the age of forty-six, he returned to a marginally improved Townsend House with his new bride, Mary Hunt, the eighteen-year-old daughter of Mary Vere Robartes and her deceased husband, Thomas Hunt, of Mollington, near Chester. Mary Hunt subsequently gave birth to three sons, Roger, Thomas and the eldest, George, who, three decades later, built Delamere Lodge.

Dorfold Hall, circa 1910: Sir Roger Wilbraham, Master of Requests to the Royal Court and brother of Richard Wilbraham of Townsend, purchased the Dorfold Hall estate in 1602.

St Mary's Parish Church, Nantwich: From 1580 many of the Wilbrahams were interred here in the family vault which now lies beneath the floor of the church. In 1858 the magnificent South Window was erected to their memory by George Fortescue Wilbraham, of Delamere House.

WILBRAHAMS OF TOWNSEND

Richard de Wilburgham
Born circa 1204, son of Richard de Wilburgham. M. (1) Margery de Vernon, eldest dtr of Warin de Vernon, (2) Letitia Venables, dtr & coheiress of Sir William Venables. Died circa 1273.

William de Wilburgham, or Wilbraham
Son of Richard de Wilburgham & Letitia Venables; born circa 1246, Radnor. Died circa 1339.

William de Wilbraham
Son born circa 1300, Radnor. Died circa 1363.

Ralph de Wilbraham
Son born circa 1340, Radnor. Died circa 1388.

William de Wilbraham
Son born circa 1300, Radnor. Died 1410.

Thomas de Wilbraham
Son, born Radnor. Died circa 1363.

Thomas de Wilbraham
Son, born circa 1389, Radnor. Married, 1401-02, Margaret dtr & heiress of John Golborne. Died circa 1470.

Randle/Randulph Wilbraham
2nd son of Thomas Wilbraham & Margaret Golborne. Died March 1498-9.

Ralph Wilbraham
Son of Randle Wilbraham. Married Elizabeth Sandford, Lancashire. Died March 7, 1552.

Richard Wilbraham
2nd son of Ralph Wilbraham. Born Aug 13, 1525. Built Townsend House, Nantwich (1575-1580). Married (1) Elizabeth, dtr of Thos. Maisterton. (2) Margaret, widow of Richard Wright of Nantwich. Died Feb 2, 1612, at Nantwich

Thomas Wilbraham
Grandson & heir of Richard Wilbraham. Born June 29, 1589. Entertained King James I at Townsend House, 1617. Married Rachel, dtr of Joshua Clive, of Huxley. Died Oct 18, 1643.

Thomas Wilbraham
2nd son & heir of Thomas Wilbraham. Born Nov 16, 1622. Died unmarr. Dec 19, 1649.

Roger Wilbraham
Heir to his brother in 1649. Born Nov 3, 1623. Sheriff of Cheshire 1669. Married Alice, dtr of Roger Wilbraham of Dorfold. Died March 15, 1707-8

Randle Wilbraham
3rd son & heir of Roger Wilbraham. Born Aug 24, 1633. Sheriff of Cheshire 1714. Married Mary, dtr of Sir Richard Brooke, of Norton. Died 1732.

Roger Wilbraham
2nd son & heir of Randle Wilbraham. Born circa 1694. Brazenose College, Dep.Lieut. of Cheshire 1725. Married (1) Elizabeth, dtr of Thomas Brooke, (2) Mary, dtr of Thomas Hunt of Mollington. Three sons, George, Roger, Thomas. Died Sept 25, 1754.

Marriage, Wealth & Inheritance

THE sudden death in childbirth of Elizabeth Brooke came to be the catalyst for the most amazing transformation in the fortunes of the Wilbraham family of Townsend. During his first marriage and though a landed gent, Roger Wilbraham's life seems to have been at a low ebb and the condition of Townsend House was perhaps symptomatic of his prevailing circumstances. Yet all was to change, dramatically and quite unexpectedly, when he took Mary Hunt, twenty-eight years his junior, to be his second wife.

Mary's mother, Mary Vere Hunt, was sister to Henry Robartes, 3rd Earl of Radnor (Cornwall), whose family seat was Lanhydrock House, near to Bodmin. The Robartes had become immensely rich from trading in wool, tin mining and money-lending, and this had enabled the family to purchase, for a huge sum, the Barony of Truro. Later the 2nd Baron Robartes of Truro, head of possibly the most affluent merchant family in the South West, was created Viscount Bodmin and Earl of Radnor. Henry, the 3rd Earl of Radnor, did not marry and when he died in 1741, less than a year after his niece's marriage to Roger Wilbraham, the Earldom descended to a kinsman. However, much of the vast Robartes' fortune, along with Lanhydrock House, passed to Mary Vere Hunt, Roger Wilbraham's mother-in-law and grandmother to young George Wilbraham and his brothers.

Mary Vere Hunt left Chester to reside at Lanhydrock and here she was surrounded by members of her immediate family, including her sons Thomas and George who, consecutively, represented Bodmin in Parliament for over thirty years. The Wilbraham family, meanwhile, continued to reside in Nantwich, at Townsend House, until the death, in 1754, of Roger Wilbraham. This left Mary a widow with three sons and she too was soon availing herself of the Robartes' hospitality. Consequently, the Wilbraham boys spent part of their childhood in

Lanhydrock House, Bodmin, the seat of the Earls of Radnor. Here, at what became the home of his grandmother, Mary Vere Hunt, George Wilbraham spent part of his childhood. Lanhydrock House is now a National Trust property.

the idyllic setting of Cornwall and from Lanhydrock House, George Wilbraham went on to Trinity College, Cambridge, though hardly had his studies commenced when, in 1758, the matriarchal Mary Vere Hunt died. Thomas and George Hunt were the major beneficiaries of Mary Vere Hunt's will, but large and handsome bequests also went to her daughters, including George's mother who seems to have promptly left Lanhydrock to return to Nantwich. Two years later she too was dead.

So at just nineteen years of age, George Wilbraham, with Mary Vere Hunt's bequest and his father's Cheshire estates, suddenly found himself richer than he could ever have imagined... and more Robartes' wealth was on the way!

George immediately assumed the responsibility of guardian to his younger brothers but the world, and particularly the attractions of London, lay at his feet. His maternal uncle George Hunt, a bachelor, owned a town house in the city, 56 Upper Seymour Street, near to Marble Arch, which was convenient for his duties as an MP at Westminster. Here young George often resided, an immensely affluent young buck immersed in the social whirl of the London season. George Hunt was undoubtedly a father-figure and when he died in 1798 he left his nephew a further enormous slice of the Robartes' money, as well as 56 Upper Seymour Street and most of the furniture and effects from Lanhydrock, the house itself having been bequeathed to a cousin, Anna Maria Hunt, who also inherited the Cornish estates. Two inventories were necessary to value the contents (excluding paintings which were considered heirlooms) of Lanhydrock and in the end Anna Maria Hunt was forced to settle an "enormous sum", exceeding £1,200, on George Wilbraham. The first valuation amounted to £670 and was clearly a shock to Anna Maria. The Lanhydrock steward wrote to her: "With respect to the appraisement of the Furniture at Lanhydrock I can only say that it much exceeded what any of us expected. At the same time I am free to say that I have heard a pleasing report of the character of the man who valued it."

Whilst residing as a young man with his uncle in Upper Seymour Street, George Wilbraham had not been a stranger in London. Numerous members of the Wilbraham family, of Cheshire, had been barristers, courtiers, important

From a painting by Battoni, George Wilbraham, the founder of Delamere Lodge, probably when he visited Italy during his Grand Tour in 1764-65.

civil servants and scholars, living and working in the capital since the 1500s; one had been the official Keeper of the Queen's Jewels, another a member of King Charles' Privy Chamber and Sir Roger Wilbraham had been Solicitor General for Ireland. To add to these ancestral antecedents, George Wilbraham was also very much part of the "Cheshire set" which, dominated by the hugely influential Grosvenors, was at the very heart of London society in the second half of the 18th century. One hundred years earlier, the Grosvenors had acquired the Manor of Ebury (much of what is now Belgravia and Mayfair) through the marriage of Sir Thomas Grosvenor to Mary Davies, the infant daughter and heiress of a City of London scrivener. Successive advancements in the peerage culminated in the dukedom of Westminster being bestowed upon the Grosvenors in 1874.

It is unclear how much time George Wilbraham actually devoted to his Cheshire estates, but there is no doubt that, with the other young men of the great Cheshire families, he often returned from the London season to enjoy months of sport on the expanding large estates and the area around Delamere Forest which offered unlimited opportunities for hunting. So, in 1762, George and his brother, Roger, were two of nine young sportsmen who founded the Tarporley Hunt Club, originally to hunt hares, rather than foxes. More than two centuries later in his outstanding book "The Green Collars", Gordon Fergusson noted:

"Whose idea it was, where it originated and what they all had in common has never been revealed, apart from their desire to indulge in the pleasures of the chase and enjoy each other's company at what was to become a regular social gathering."

It would appear that George's passion for hunting and riding, and the formation of the Tarporley Hunt Club, was one of the reasons for him commencing to sever his direct ties with Nantwich and South Cheshire. Townsend House was in terminal decline during his father's time and, without the parental incumbecies of his young friends who were largely 'heirs-in-waiting', George possessed the wealth and independence to establish his own hunting lodge. He therefore turned his attention to Hefferston Grange, Weaverham, a large property that had become vacant and was available on lease.

Mentioned in Domesday, Hefferston Grange had been the site of one of the Abbot of Vale Royal's grange farms and, after the Dissolution of the Monasteries, passed via the Holcrofts to the Warburton family. The house had been rebuilt early in the 18th century and here, until his death in 1760, the keen sportsman Philip Henry Warburton maintained a private pack of hounds. Hefferston Grange, located in the centre of hunting country and with stabling and kennels, must have seemed ideal for George Wilbraham and at the formation of the Tarporley Hunt Club, in 1762, his address was, significantly, recorded as "The Grange, Weaverham".

Crucially, Hefferston Grange was close to the Manor of Crowton (3) which was an important consideration when George Wilbraham decided to settle permanently in the district. The Ardernes held three-quarters of Crowton Manor, including Crowton Hall and the Crowton Chapel in Weaverham Parish Church. All this George Wilbraham purchased from John Arderne in 1789 and later his grandson completed the whole by acquiring the fourth share from the descendants of Ralph Leycester. George Wilbraham may also have had an interest in the Forest of Delamere through the marriage of his 16th century ancestor, Dorothy Wilbraham, of Woodhey, to Sir John Done, the Master Forester. The

Hefferston Grange, built for Philip Henry Warburton in 1741. George Wilbraham was leasing the property at the founding of the Tarporley Hunt Club and this was his Cheshire home until he erected Delamere Lodge.

A Tarporley Hunt Club Meet at The Swan.

Wilbraham connection is reinforced in a document from 1626 stating that Sir John "... enjoyed the living of pigs, pasture, herbage and pannage for the lifetime of himself, his son and Sir Richard Wilbraham".

It is a matter of conjecture as to precisely which land George directly owned in Cuddington and Crowton and the available records within the public domain are confusing, though it is worthy of mention that as late as the 18th century parish and manorial boundaries were often blurred. The land (Delamere Park) of Yeoman John Done, mentioned in the 1660 parchment, abutted the meeting point of the parishes of Cuddington, Crowton and Norley and this passed to George Wilbraham, though whether through purchase or inheritance it is impossible to establish.

The Wilbraham Diary does not cover George Wilbraham's life between 1762 and 1784 and there are only fragments of information concerning his lifestyle, alternating as it must have done between his uncle's London home and Hefferston Grange. What is certain is that whilst resident in Cheshire, George immersed himself in the affairs of the Tarporley Hunt Club, serving as President in 1770 and Hunt Secretary in 1773. He also features prominently in the records of the Hunt Club Races which informally commenced in 1774 and his name regularly appeared amongst the owners, as in November 1882: "Tuesday last on Crabtree Green the Tarporley Sweepstakes were run for 10 guineas each, 1 four mile heat, each horse to carry 12 stone. Won by Lord Stamford's mare Diana.". George Wilbraham's mare, Cull, was fourth.

Cheshire's principal race meetings at the time were at Chester, Farndon, Knutsford and Wallasey, but there was also a long-established course at Crabtree Green, on land owned by George Wilbraham. Crabtree Green Races, as the fixture became known, was a colourful occasion and by 1805 there is even mention, in Hunt Club minutes, of a grandstand on the course which was located on either side of Stonyford Lane. The last race meeting at Crabtree Green took place in November 1815, two years after George Wilbraham's death, apparently due to the Crown enclosure of Delamere Forest. The fixture continued, until the beginning of the Second World War, as the annual Tarporley Hunt Steeplechases, latterly on a permanent course, established in 1877 on Arderne Estate land at Tarporley.

George Wilbraham was obviously a busy and active young man during the decades of the 1760s and 1770s and, as was customary amongst his affluent contemporaries, he embarked upon the Grand Continental Tour, visiting France, Italy, Turkey, Greece and the Levant. At the age of thirty-three, in 1774, he then married Maria Harvey, of Essex, the second daughter of the both deceased William and Emma Harvey. Maria's aunt was the wife of a Grosvenor and it was almost

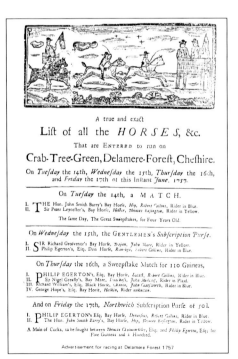

Crabtree Green racecourse is marked on a 17th century map and this notice dates from 1757. The Tarporley Hunt Club staged meetings here, "on George Wilbraham's land" 1774-1815.

Rolls Park, Chigwell, the home of Maria Harvey's family.

certainly through the Grosvenors that the couple were introduced.

Though not on the grand scale of the Robartes, of Lanhydrock House, the Harveys, of Rolls Park, Chigwell, were also wealthy from a fortune founded on merchant trading, as well as business interests in the City of London. Maria's father, William Harvey (1714-63), had fought with the Jacobites in Bonny Prince Charlie's army at the Battle of Culloden and one of his five sons, Maria's brother, was Eliab Harvey who, during the Battle of Trafalgar, captained the 98-gun "Temeraire", later immortalised by J.M.W.Turner in his painting, "The Fighting Temeraire". As Admiral Sir Eliab Harvey he served as an MP for Essex for over thirty years and also became a close friend to his brother-in-law, George Wilbraham, for whom he later acted as an executor to his will.

When George moved his bride into Hefferston Grange, in 1774, the countryside of England, including Cheshire, was in the throes of unprecedented social and economic change, brought about by the iniquitous Enclosure Acts, private Acts of Parliament absurdly titled "Enclosure Awards", which swept aside the feudal rights of the little man, the cottager, the tenement-holder who survived on the few strips of earth around the waste lands not in possession of the inheritors of the original Norman lords. Nationally, between 1700 and 1844, almost seven million acres fell under Enclosure Acts, what "The Enclosure Man of England and Wales 1595-1918" describes as "... an instrument of land re-organisation and control which both reflected and consolidated the power of those who commissioned them".

Cheshire was, in a sense, different from much of the rest of the nation and little of its overall acreage fell to Parliamentary Enclosure, due in no small measure to the fact that, in the 18th century, there were 143 family seats of the nobility and gentry spread across the county. These landowning lords, who already held the best, the most fertile ground, now saw rich pickings in the commons and wastes as a means of extending their estates for the production of food for the expanding industrial towns. They did not want small independent freeholders with bits of land in the

Admiral Sir Eliab Harvey, George Wilbraham's brother-in-law, who captained the famous "Temeraire" in the Battle of Trafalgar.

midst of their estates, or in possession of cottages, or cultivated patches won out of the wastes, or entitled to keep a few head of cattle on the open commons.

Locally, the major landowners were the Smith-Barrys, of Marbury; the Ardernes, of Arden (Tarporley); the Egertons, of Oulton; and the Cholmondeleys, of Vale Royal. Richard Smith-Barry, John Arderne and Francis Welles, of Sandbach, claimed the inheritance of shares in the "Fee of Kingsley" with its twelve manors, including Norley, Cuddington, Crowton and Onston. The Arderne Papers, preserved at the Cheshire Record Office, paint a vivid picture of the collusiveness of the major estate owners in respect of the waste lands and in June, 1758, Smith-Barry's agent wrote to Arderne's agent requesting a meeting to examine the extent of encroachments on the commons and, if necessary, to pull down offending cottages and eject the transgressors... "and after to adjourn to Weaverham where I shou'd be glad if you wou'd take a little dinner with me"!

At Knutsford, two years later, the large estate owners attended a meeting arranged by James Tomkinson, an astute lawyer who, it is difficult to believe otherwise, was acting on behalf of George Wilbraham. Operating out of Welsh Row, Nantwich, Tomkinson had a reputation as a clever legal man, but "grasping and parsimonious" and for many years his hand had been on the tiller of the affairs of various Wilbrahams. Indeed, it is said that whilst managing those of George Wilbraham's kinsman, Roger Wilbraham, he deliberately allowed the Dorfold Hall (Nantwich) estate to spiral into financial meltdown, so enabling him to personally acquire it at a vastly reduced price. It was entirely possible he was also running George Wilbraham's estates in Cheshire and, if so, he would certainly have had a vested interest in ensuring the smooth passage of any Enclosure movement that may have impacted on land in which George Wilbraham was interested.

The object of the gathering at Knutsford was to further promote a proposal to enclose, by Act of Parliament, "the wasts in dispute near Norley and Crowton" and, as the estate owners were steadfast in their conviction that they owned these lands, Tomkinson's invitation was guaranteed to strike a chord... "It will I believe be a very considerable advantage to the Gentlemen who are chiefly interested in thos wasts". In fact, the gentlemen conveniently overlooked that the wastes of Norley, and Crowton, as well as

George Wilbraham's wife, Maria Harvey (1755-1822). A portrait by Daniel Gardner.

those of Kingsley and Cuddington, were, first and foremost, King's land, i.e. Delamere Forest. It is true that these villages and their wastes had once been within the Norman's Fee of Kingsley, but through marital sub-divisions over centuries, the ancient titles and rights had been dissipated and following the Civil War and Restoration there was no-one to challenge the power of Smith Barry, Arderne and Welles. Indeed, there is little doubt that the wastes should have remained open common until Delamere Forest came to be enclosed by the Crown fifty years later.

Tomkinson was clearly the prime mover, the legal conduit, for local Enclosure and he would have argued, as others had done elsewhere, that "... the said commons are of little value, but if divided into specific allotments and enclosed, the same might be considerably improved, whereby a manifest advantage would ensue to the several persons interested therein".

As it turned out, it was not the commons of Norley and Crowton that first fell to Tomkinson's Enclosure, but Bryn Common, Cuddington. Early maps show wider Cuddington principally divided into tenements supported by the "waste" of Bryn Common which covered much of the area upon which the modern village has been developed, i.e. north-west from the Chester-Manchester road, at Blakemere, towards Small Brook and the boundary with Norley, though well clear of the Cuddington plateau and the fertile land of the Dones. In 1767, the Cuddington Enclosure Act was enacted, to enclose 460 acres of Bryn Common and this, with the enclosure ten years later of the Kingsley, Norley and Crowton commons, had a major bearing upon George Wilbraham's plans to build his own hunting lodge estate on the former Done land, near to the "Townfield", of Cuddington.

The general upheaval created by the Enclosures is well documented and in the specific case of Bryn Common, hardly surprisingly, the three principal beneficiaries were allocated the majority of the 460 acres. To make matters even more advantageous, George Wilbraham was a willing buyer, anxious to exchange his South Cheshire property, almost certainly to Tomkinson, so that he could acquire as much land as possible around Cuddington, Crowton and Norley, the greater part of it once King's land.

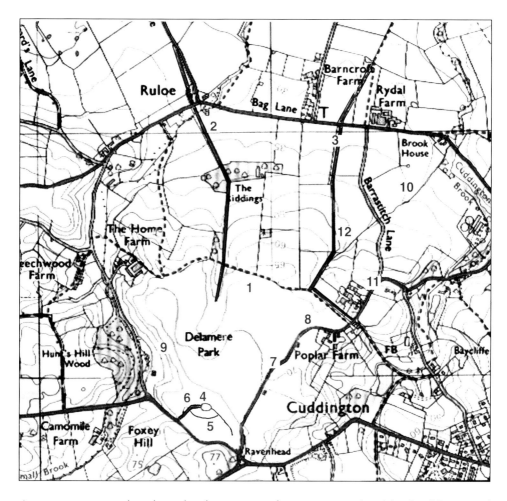

A contour map showing the important sites connected with the history of Delamere Park and Cuddington village. Some of the modern locations have been retained to assist with identification: 1. Land "claimed" by the Dones in the 1660 parchment; 2. Cart road closed by the Dones in 1660; 3. Cart road given by the Dones in 1660; 4. Contour showing the mound of the "Captain's Tree"; 5. Old House Meadow; 6. Site of "Time Team" dig in 2000; 7. Walker's Croft; 8. Buckley's Croft; 9. Long Shoot Croft; 10. Samuel Youd's ditch, later called Barry's Ditch, now corrupted to Barrastitch; 11. Well, opposite to the entrance of what is now Cuddington Hall Farm; 12. Sluice, aquifer outlet.

Wyatt's House on the Hill

.... he hired a place in the neighbourhood called the Grange
where he resided for several years about the year 1784 and
subsequently he bought various farms and land bordering on the
forest of Delamere and built, after a plan by Wyatt, the house
which we now occupy.

- The Wilbraham Diary

THOUGH still a relatively young man, George Wilbraham enjoyed great wealth and status in Cheshire and following his marriage to Maria Harvey it was natural, in keeping with others of the landed gentry who orientated towards the Tarporley hunting fields, that he should have turned to creating his own country estate. Townsend House, the old family seat at Nantwich, and Weaver Hall, with its thousand acres south of the River Weaver, were both within comfortable riding distance of Tarporley, but neither could have held much appeal. Townsend House, in a ruinous condition, was wholly inappropriate, whilst Weaver Hall, though perhaps marginally more preferable due to its rural location, was far too close to the belching chimneys and pollution of the Winsford salthouses.

George Wilbraham wanted his new family seat to be a statement, somewhere imposing and squirearchal; a hunting lodge to see and be seen. And where better than on part of the former Done lands, on the highest ground overlooking Cuddington, Crowton, Weaverham and Delamere Forest? George's house, fittingly titled "Delamere Lodge", would stand high and proud and not

Walker's Croft, typical 18th century village dwellings, on Park Lane (Cuddington Lane). These became tied-workers' cottages acquired by the Wilbrahams, their occupants' feudal rights effectively swept away by the Enclosure of Bryn Common.

for a moment did he ever rationalise it as being sited in Cudddington. From first occupant to last, the Wilbrahams always considered themselves resident in Delamere Forest and Crowton.

For years George had been reorganising and consolidating, disposing of property in the south of the county, much of it to the "clever lawyer" James Tomkinson, and purchasing land around Crowton and Cuddington, including most of the Bryn Common Enclosure allotments of Smith Barry, Arderne and Welles. It was a programme of acquisition he continued until the start of the 19th century.

To design Delamere Lodge, George Wilbraham engaged Samuel Wyatt (1737-1807), an architectural radical whose works during an eminent career included Trinity House and the Longships, Dungeness and Flamborough Head lighthouses. Wyatt also specialised in designing country houses/hunting lodges and amongst his commissions in Cheshire were Bostock Hall (1775), for Edward Tomkinson; Hooton Hall (1778), for Sir William Stanley, and Doddington Hall (1776-1800) for Sir Thomas Broughton. He redesigned Tatton Hall, Knutsford and reconstructed (1782) Penrhyn Castle, Bangor, for Lord Penrhyn who also owned Winnington Hall, Northwich, to which was added the striking "Wyatt wing".

One of the most enterprising architects of his time in the handling of geometrical space, Wyatt's favourite design is grandly described as a "harmonious synthesis of cubes and semi-circles", often incorporating characteristics such as "domed bows, looking like tea canisters". In his younger days at Kedleston Hall, Derbyshire, he had been employed as a carpenter by the architect and designer, Robert Adam, and at both Delamere Lodge and Doddington he replicated Kedleston's central copper-domed bow, flanked by over-arched tripartite windows, with decorative panels, or Coades stone plaques, examples of which can still be seen in his work at Tatton. It is possible the copper domes were manufactured by the great industrialist Matthew Boulton with whom Wyatt was closely associated.

Approaching the peak of his career and based in London at the time of building Delamere Lodge, Wyatt must have been overseeing many major projects nationally and it is doubtful that he made more than fleeting visits to check on progress in Cheshire. He often used granite in the construction of his country houses and George Wilbraham, possibly through West Country family links with the Robartes, of Lanhydrock, or the Harveys, acquired in excess of two-hundred tons of Exmoor granite with which to build the main part of Delamere Lodge. Shipped from Devon to the busy little port of Frodsham, the granite would have been conveyed in barges up the River Weaver to Pickerings Wharf, below Crowton. Due to the depth of the river at this time, the maximum weight carried by a single barge was just three tons, so at least sixty barge-loads of stone would have arrived at Pickerings, all manhandled onto carts for the final leg of the journey, along "Ainsworth Lane" and "Bent Lane" to the Delamere Lodge building site high on the hill.

Samuel Wyatt, the architectural radical who designed Delamere Lodge for George Wilbraham.

The principal part of Delamere Lodge, i.e. the front facing to the East, was exclusively constructed of Exmoor granite and the illustrations of Doddington Hall and another Wyatt design, Coton House, Warwickshire (1784), probably best reflect what the original looked like. Major alterations during the tenure of George Wilbraham's son and grandson significantly altered the overall external appearance of Delamere Lodge and text descriptions from the 19th and 20th centuries all refer to the later remodelled house.

Behind the Exmoor granite facade, on a line East to West, was the largest part of the house, the West Wing, and, intriguingly, this was constructed of locally-made brick. It is impossible to determine whether this was a deviation from Wyatt's plan, but what we do know is that a "Brickfield" is marked on early maps, to the rear of the modern, refurbished "Tank Shed". Brick-making in the 19th century was a rough and ready process and, using clay from

Similar to Delamere Lodge, Doddington Hall, near Nantwich (top) and Coton Hall, Warwickshire, were "hunting lodges" designed by Samuel Wyatt, with domed bow frontages "looking like tea canisters". The Coade stone plaques can clearly be seen on Doddington.

Cuddington Waste, the firing would have been at relatively low temperatures, so producing what modern brickmakers would consider an extremely soft and low-grade product. It is likely that these locally-made bricks formed part of the structure of Delamere Lodge's West Wing and, ultimately, contributed to the decline and demise of the building 150 years later.

The West Wing brickwork was laid in a strong Flemish bond and a photographic cross-section shows a low-pitched and linear roof with three large spans supported by two external and two internal walls. These walls were not, however, supported with piers, although it was common to insert large lengths of timber to provide additional horizontal strength to the brickwork. If, as seems likely, the house later suffered from dry rot then these timbers may have become a critical weakness.

The 1839 Tithe Map indicates three additional structures connected with the original house, i.e. Orangery, Conservatory and Pavilion. The cultivation of orange plants had been popular since the 17th century and the large garden buildings, required to house the pots, would often be transformed during the

George Wilbraham's house with the copper dome and decorative Coade stone plaques (garlands of oak leaves). This photograph dates from the turn of the 20th century and shows the main entrance located on the North side. A large window has replaced the original East entrance built by Samuel Wyatt. The South Drive, culminating at the ornate gate, was realigned in the 19th century, either by George Wilbraham's son, or by his grandson.

summer months for the staging of social functions. Orangeries became a fashion statement and Wyatt frequently included them within the main fabric of his houses. The Delamere Lodge Orangery was probably a brick construction with a solid roof and it appears to have been semi-circular in shape.

George Wilbraham's Conservatory, measuring 200 square feet, was large by anyone's standards in a period when such structures were an essential feature of the very best country houses, but whether constructed of brick, or essentially metal-framed, it is impossible to determine, though Wyatt was certainly in the vanguard where use of cast-iron was concerned. His iron columns on a building in the grounds of Winnington Hall (circa 1782-85) are among the earliest known. The high maintenance that conservatories required meant that many early versions were abandoned and this was certainly the case at Delamere Lodge, approximately fifty years later.

Internally, the fluted alcoves and octagonal rooms at Delamere matched Wyatt's designs at Winnington Hall and Tatton. The original front entrance opened into what was a relatively small hallway containing an early version of a Wyatt cantilevered staircase, beneath which was a set of tubular bells used as dinner gongs. Also on the ground floor of the curved granite frontage was the dining room and library, whilst through the centre of the West Wing ran an exceptionally wide corridor, with a large drawing room facing to the south. On the other side of this corridor, facing north, would have been George Wilbraham's study and smoking room, or billiard room, where he probably regaled his hunting friends. The kitchens and service rooms were at the far end of the corridor. The upper floor incorporated the principal bedrooms and in the West Wing, on a sliding scale of master-servant, were further bedrooms, a nursery, a music room and the servants' quarters.

Delamere Lodge was surrounded by two-hundred acres of open pastureland with a carriage drive crossing it from the then Town Lane, the entrance to which was midway between modern Hollow Oak Lane and the Wilbraham Gate. Beyond Delamere Lodge, the drive continued down to Woods Lane and the newly-constructed Home Farm which may also have been designed by Samuel Wyatt.

The Wilbraham Diary states that George and his wife Maria moved into Delamere Lodge "about the year 1784" and this is confirmed in baptismal records for St Mary's Church, Weaverham. George Wilbraham leased Hefferston Grange for an extraordinarily lengthy period, around twenty years, and six of his eight children were born here, or were living here at the time of their baptisms. The Bishop of Chester's transcripts show that George and Maria's first-born son, Roger, died in February 1784, at the age of seven, and two months later, on April 24th, 1784, the baptism took place of Elizabeth "... daughter of George Wilbraham Esq of the Grange by Maria". Significantly, Elizabeth was the last of the Wilbraham births recorded from Hefferston

Grange. Her younger sibling, Louisa, was baptised on September 12, 1786, by which time George and Maria's address was listed as "Delamere Lodge". This conclusively places George and Maria Wilbraham moving into their new home between April 24, 1784 and September 12, 1786.

George Wilbraham settled into the life of a country gentleman and quickly introduced new methods of farming to the large open fields, including horse-powered machinery, crop rotation, shippons with concrete floors, separate stalls for calving and Dutch barns for storing hay. Meanwhile the tenement holders, thirty-six on Wilbraham land, who had previously enjoyed feudal rights on the old common, became tied workers on the estate. The ever-expanding industrial towns were placing great demands upon agriculture and George Wilbraham's model farming techniques attracted interest from far and wide.

Farming, hunting and local administrative duties fully occupied George Wilbraham, though, in 1789, he agreed to become a Member of Parliament for Bodmin. His maternal uncles George, and later, Thomas Hunt had represented

George and Maria Wilbraham had eight children and here are the eldest, born 1775 and 1776, Maria and Emma, from a painting by Daniel Gardner. George and Maria's first-born son Roger died in 1784, aged seven. The other children were: George, 1779; William, 1781; Elizabeth, 1784; Louisa, 1786 and Anna, 1791. Only Louisa and Anna were born at Delamere Lodge.

the Cornish borough since 1747 at a time when Parliamentary seats were simply passed to another family member. George Wilbraham did not enjoy life at Westminster and found it "inconvenient to quit his family and home as often as his Parliamentary duties required" and at the next election, one year later, he stood down in favour of his brother Roger who had previously been an MP for Helston. In his short career at Westminster, George was probably present when William Wilberforce made his historic first speech, a three-hour epic, in May 1789, on the abolition of slavery.

George Wilbraham served as a Sheriff of Chester and a local magistrate but gave up hunting, and retired from the Tarporley Hunt Club, when badly afflicted with gout and asthma. His death occurred at Delamere Lodge on December 3, 1813, and his remains were interred in the family vault at Nantwich Church. His eldest surviving son, George Wilbraham (1779 – 1852), inherited and large sums of money were bequeathed to his daughters, Emma, Elizabeth and Anne, and to his youngest son, William "... now a captain in His Majesty's navy".

Lysons "Cheshire", 1810, said of George Wilbraham at the time of his death: "... few men have passed through life with a more unsullied reputation. He was of a modest and unambitious nature and, though well versed in his earlier years in those languages and studies which form an accomplished gentleman, he chose rather as he advanced in age to addict himself to those pursuits which are practically useful to mankind, so that he left behind him the reputation of an enlightened agriculturist, a kind landlord and master and an affectionate and respected parent."

Maria, George's widow, faired less well than her children, but not through any lack of affection. A codicil to George's will reveals he had sold his house in London, 56 Upper Seymour Street, and replaced it with a property in "Mickledale Tenement". At one of these addresses, Sarah Harriet Burney, who was to become one of the most famous novelists of the early 19th century, is recorded as "working as governess to the daughters of George Wilbraham (1741-1813)". George left the Mickledale Tenement property and its contents to his "dear wife" and also the "coach and chaise, four coach-horses and harness, and the horse she most usually rides". Ironically this very "chaise" might have contributed to Maria's own death nine years later when she was residing with her daughters in one of the estate lodges at the Harvey family seat, Rolls Park, in Chigwell, Essex. During an afternoon drive through Hainault Forest, in September 1822, Maria and her second daughter Elizabeth were involved in a terrible accident, as outlined in extracts from letters written by Lady Louisa Harvey, the wife of Admiral Sir Eliab Harvey, to her own daughter, Louisa Lloyd, of Aston Hall, Oswestry:

> I am very much afraid your poor Aunt Wilbraham will not survive the frightful accident she met with today, this morning, at one o'clock. It is now ten and she has been insensible ever since. Copeland (the Harvey doctor) thinks she had fractured her scull (sic) – we are all in great distress. This morning she went out as usual with Eliz W. in a little four wheel'd chaise driven by her Footman, on going down the Hill on the other side of Hog Hill, the Shaft broke, the Horse reared violently, the Coachman fell off, the Horse ran away, and your poor Aunt was either thrown out or scrambled out, fell on the back of her head, Eliza also hump'd out, hurt her head in the same place, no one being near, they lay (at least yr Aunt and the Coachman) lay a long time without assistance by the side of the road.... Dr Holland by his manner does not think Mrs Wilbraham can recover.

Maria Wilbraham, the woman who had borne George Wilbraham's eight children and who had done so much with him to create Delamere Lodge, died two days later. Lady Louisa Harvey wrote:

> Eliza is getting better. I can never forget the scene in the Forest, nor its subsequent consequences. Re Maria's will: The London House of course returns to George. She leaves all to the girls she has, and requests to be taken to Nantwich leaving £200 for her burial. The Coroner was obliged to take an inquest yesterday on account of the accident.

Maria was duly interred alongside her husband in the Nantwich family vault on September 23, 1822, by which time a second astonishing chapter was beginning to unfold at Delamere Lodge.

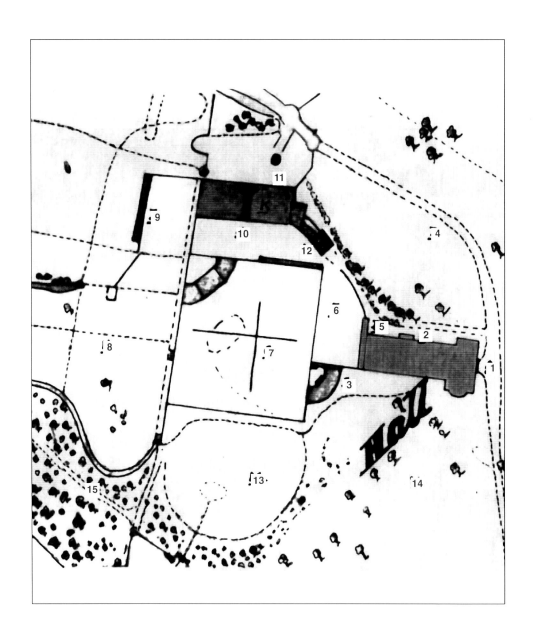

On the adjoining page is an enlarged extract from the 1839 Tithe Map for Cuddington, showing the first detailed plan of the original Delamere Lodge. When this plan was actually surveyed is unknown since it appears to have been overlaid, as stated previously, on an earlier map. The most significant features are:

1. The entrance to the house is at the front, facing East, with the drive sweeping up to it. This is typical of Samuel Wyatt's Hunting Lodge design.
2. A second, lesser, entrance on the North side.
3. Pavilion with rear entrance.
4. From the front door the drive continues to the rear of the stables and coach house, and then passes the Home Farm to Woods Lane and Norley.
5. A road and paths run from the drive along the North side of the house and onto the Stables.
6. Almost certainly the Orangery.
7. Conservatory, 200-feet square, with architects' crossed lines, indicating a roof.
8. Possibly a partially-walled exercise paddock for hounds.
9. Most likely the kennels.
10. Typical stable yard.
11. Possibly the Clock Tower.
12. Coach House and Stables.
13. Main lawn, south of the Conservatory and surrounded by trees.
14. Open parkland.
15. Woodland path along top of the valley above Woods Lane; survived until modern housing development neared completion.

Politics & Blue Blood

SINCE the 13th century when Richard de Wilburgham had plighted his troth to daughters of the Verdins and Venables, successive heads of the Wilbrahams married exceedingly well, each heir, each generation, unfailingly elevating the family's status and wealth. By far the most spectacularly beneficial had been Roger Wilbraham's second marriage into the Robartes' commercial fortune, a large share of which passed to George Wilbraham, the founder of Delamere Lodge. However, it was George's son who took the family to new, previously unthinkable horizons and the very highest echelons of society.

Born at Hefferston Grange in 1779, the second George Wilbraham was educated at Rugby School and spent two years at Trinity College, Cambridge, the latter an exercise which, as he notes in the Wilbraham Diary, was hardly successful:

> I remained at the university little more than two years, and not profiting much by the instructions of my tutors, or by the discipline of that learned body, I took a commission in the Cheshire Militia then at Winchester. In 1799 I was induced to purchase a commission in the army and served as Lieutenant in the King's Own Regiment of Infantry during the campaign in North Holland.

The Dutch campaign, fought against France and Belgium, concluded in 1802 and, in spite of Europe remaining a hotbed of unrest and intrigue, George set off to tour France, an adventure he would never forget.

> Being at liberty to indulge my taste for foreign travel I went to France where I was presented to Napoleon Bonaparte then 1st Consul of the French Republic. After travelling through France I

returned to Paris and there became one of the victims of that awful edict of the French Governor which considered Prisoners all the English within their grasp. I spent part of my captivity at Verdun, but no inconsiderable portion of it at Paris. I was however fortunate enough to be permitted to come home in 1806.

Strong shield: Crest of the Fortescues.

The four years of their son's imprisonment must have placed a terrible strain on his parents and when he finally reached Delamere Lodge they would, no doubt, have been pressing him to settle down, to find himself a wife and take over management of the estates from his father whose health was noticeably deteriorating. Young George would become extremely wealthy upon his inheritance and through the family's extensive London connections he was introduced to his future wife, Lady Anne Fortescue, a daughter of Hugh, Viscount Ebrington, the 1st Earl of Fortescue, of Castle Hill, a palatial mansion in the Devon village of Filleigh, near Barnstaple.

The Fortescues were directly descended from the Norman, Richard Le Fort who was at the Battle of Hastings in 1066. The legend is that Richard used his shield to save William, the Duke of Normandy, and consequently adopted the name Fort Escu (Strong Shield). His son, Adam, settled in South Devon and the Fortescues stood at the pinnacle of aristocracy in the South West of England.

Lady Anne was a grand-daughter of George Grenville and her great-uncle had been William Pitt (the Elder), both British Prime Ministers in the 1760s. One of her uncles, Lord William Wyndham Grenville, was Prime Minister in 1806-7 and another, George Nugent Temple Grenville, was the First Marquess of Buckingham. Other close relatives included the Earls of Devon, Portsmouth and Harrowby, Baron Carysfort (Ireland) and Baron Braybrooke.

However, it was through Lady Anne's grandmother, Elizabeth Wyndham (wife of George Grenville) that all future Wilbrahams, of the Delamere Lodge line, may be traced to nothing less than the very birth of the Tudor monarchy. Elizabeth Wyndham was a daughter of Charles Seymour, 6th Duke of Somerset,

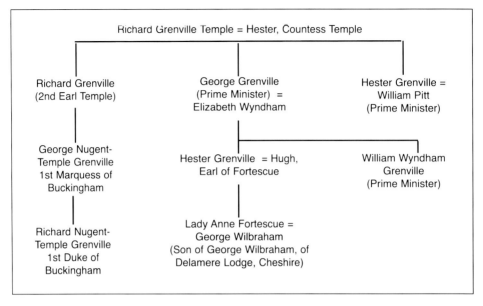

The Grenville Temple lineage into which George Wilbraham married.

and Lady Elizabeth Percy, a daughter of the 11th Earl of Northumberland. The lineage of the Dukes of Somerset, through the Beauforts and Seymours, is engrained in English history as far back as John O'Gaunt, the third son of King Edward III and younger brother to the Black Prince. The name most associated with the Seymours is, of course, Jane Seymour, the third wife of Henry VIII, who died after giving birth to Edward VI. Through Elizabeth Wyndham's maternal Percy line and the Dukes of Northumberland, Lady Anne Fortescue's ancestors notably included Sir Henry Percy, "Hotspur" of Shakespearean renown, who was killed at the Battle of Shrewsbury in 1403.

Breeding and reputation were everything within the aristocracy and the Wilbrahams of Delamere Lodge operated on a social strata infinitely inferior to the Fortescues and, whatever it may have developed into later, this seems to have been a marriage of convenience. As far as the Wilbrahams were concerned, the union of Lady Anne and George was a glittering appendage to their prestige and standing, particularly beyond the confines of Cheshire, whilst the daughters of the Earl & Countess of Fortescue were, naturally, expected to marry well, if not for title then for wealth... and George Wilbraham, with his father's inheritances from the Robartes' fortune, possessed wealth in abundance.

George Wilbraham succeeded his father in December, 1813, and in the following September, 1814, he married Lady Anne, at Filleigh, but not before agreeing to a comprehensive marriage settlement, to prove his worth to the Fortescues. The marriage settlement document extended to almost one-hundred pages and detailed every cottage, tenement and building, every acre, rood, perch, rent and church pew owned by the Wilbrahams in Cheshire. Lady Anne, the Earl & Countess of Fortescue, Richard Temple Grenville-Nugent (Second Marquess and later First Duke of Buckingham), and George's uncle, Roger Wilbraham MP, were the trustees of this settlement which also served as a tax-avoidance measure to counter "legacy and succession duty" imposed, ironically, during the Prime Ministership of Lady Anne's second cousin, William Pitt, the Younger. Signed and sealed two weeks prior to the wedding, the most striking

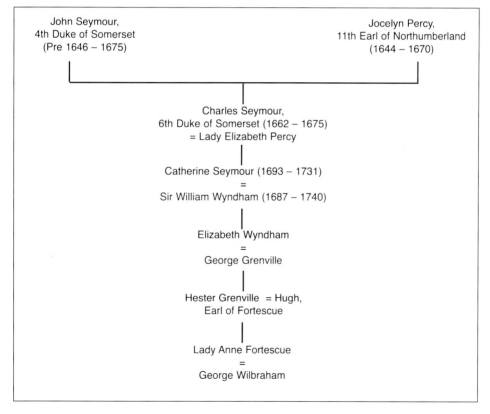

The Seymour-Percy lineage into which George Wilbraham married.

55

George Wilbraham MP, by Hayter as part of his study for his famous Parliamentary painting of the Great Reform debate.

feature of the marriage was the absence of any dowry and that Lady Anne Fortescue added only her name to the bargain.

Lady Anne was undoubtedly a formidable young woman and once George's mother, Maria, had been summarily packed off to Essex, she quickly asserted herself as the new mistress of Delamere Lodge which, by her standards, bore not the slightest comparison with the sumptuous surroundings to which she was accustomed, at Castle Hill, Devon, and the other great aristocratic houses she had frequented. In short, Delamere Lodge must have seemed to her a dreary place; bad enough that it was in the North; worse, it had been designed as a country gentleman's hunting lodge.

Putting duty first however, Lady Anne endured a period of almost continuous pregnancy leading to the birth of five sons, the first of whom was George Fortescue Wilbraham, born in August 1815. At Delamere Lodge, Lady Anne played her part as mistress, wife and mother, but when the opportunity arose for her husband to enter into politics she was probably delighted. London and the London high-life beckoned!

It was the Grosvenors, and probably Lady Anne's family connections, who steered George Wilbraham towards politics and in 1826 he was elected one of two MPs for Stockbridge, in Hampshire, a notorious "rotten borough" where candidates openly bribed electors at a going rate in excess of 70 guineas per head. The senior MP for Stockbridge was General (later Field Marshall) Tom Grosvenor, a nephew of Lord Grosvenor. Tom Grosvenor had previously been thirty years an MP for Chester and while George Wilbraham was contemplating the first rungs on the political ladder, the General was drifting towards retirement. Together they represented Stockbridge until 1831 when Tom Grosvenor, at the age of sixty-six, announced he was taking George's sister, Anne, twenty years younger, as his second wife.

Tom Grosvenor wrote to the Duke of Rutland: "I cannot live alone. And I have been so fortunate as to find a gentle lady that takes pity on my singleness. She is the younger sister of George Wilbraham, already my cousin, so that we have no new connexions, no new faces to cultivate... The fact is I have done with all politics & public men and measures. I shall shut my eyes to all newspapers And I must open them on something".

Castle Hill, the palatial home, in Devon, of the Fortescues.

Lady Anne, watercolour (1837) by J.Holmes.

Lord Grosvenor's wife severely disapproved of Anne Wilbraham: "She is.... said to be an old maid, disagreeable, cross and peevish. I think they are both crazy". However, Lady Grosvenor later agreed that the General and his wife did get on well together, even if the lady was a bore!

George Wilbraham was a Whig and in his maiden speech to Parliament he spoke in favour of the repeal of the Test Act which barred Catholics from high public office. He also frequently debated on constitutional matters, notably during passage of the Reform Act, of 1832, by which time he had become an MP for Chester. In the 1831 election, George Wilbraham and Lord Belgrave were unopposed in Chester and, following speeches of thanks in front of 10,000 in the Castle yard, they were both placed in ceremonial chairs and conveyed in triumph to the Royal Hotel where a dinner was provided for the Sheriff and friends. Elsewhere, in inns and taverns around the city, some 2,000 dinners, and a bottle of wine apiece, were provided for the freeholders.

Between 1833 and 1841, George Wilbraham represented Cheshire South and altogether, during a political career spanning fifteen years, he witnessed the comings and goings of six prime ministers, including the Duke of Wellington, Earl Grey, Viscount Melbourne and Sir Robert Peel.

The 1831 Chester election had been fortunate for George Wilbraham as, more often than not, fearsome campaigns prevailed. In 1837, when standing for the first Parliament of Queen Victoria's reign, he found himself pitched with Sir Philip Grey-Egerton, of Oulton, against the unpopular Edwin

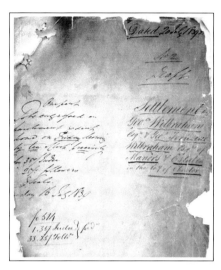

The Deed of Marriage Settlement by which George Wilbraham proved his wealth to the Fortescues.

Corbett, Squire of Darnhall Grange, Winsford. A poster survives from this contest and it demonstrates that no political quarter was given, even to a fellow county gentleman:

> Men of Cheshire, your old and valued friend Mr Wilbraham has been unexpectedly menaced by an opposition to his re-election by Mr Corbett, of Darnhall, backed by the king of Hanover, the Carlton Club and the Hoo-Green Clique of Cheshire. The Gentle Edwin has been lured from the classic shades of Darnhall to wend his way to the three-cornered room at Northwich, clothed with the armour of bigotry and intolerance, like a second Don Quixote, to attack your independence, and, if possible, to prostrate it altogether. If anything could win your votes from the cause of Freedom and Reform, the bland and conciliating manners of Mr Corbett would certainly effect it, who has a smile of benevolence and good humour to greet everyone who accosts him. But electors remember that under this genial appearance there may lurk the savage and morose magistrate, the abettor of every arbitrary and unpopular measure that ever emanated from a bench of Cheshire magistrates, and, to crown all, there may exist under this exterior the determined foe of civil and religious liberty. Ponder well before you trust such a man. Principle and gratitude ought alike to induce you to vote for Geo. Wilbraham.

Needless to say, this was long before the days of libel laws and George Wilbraham was using every trick to vent his spleen on Squire Corbett who, some years previously, had been involved in a highly charged poaching affair centred upon Darnhall Grange and Nantwich. George was cleverly resurrecting this unsavoury episode and when the Squire attended election meetings he was constantly mocked with dead pheasants, hoisted on poles and waved before his face. George Wilbraham's impassioned plea worked the oracle and, on August 8, 1837, he was returned, with Sir Philip Grey-Egerton, to represent Cheshire South. Corbett trailed in a distant third and when the result was announced, in Nantwich, he was forced to make his escape by swimming across the river. Four years later and finding himself in a minority to Sir Robert Peel's Tory government, George Wilbraham retired from politics.

Whilst serving as a Member of Parliament it ideally suited George and Lady Anne to reside in London, only returning to Delamere during the seasonal migrations based upon Parliamentary recesses. Furtherance of her husband's political career, the London season and high society were what mattered most to Lady Anne and to this end the former city-base of

The 1837 General Election poster with George Wilbraham's vitriolic attack on Squire Corbett, of Darnhall.

George's father, Mickledale Tenement, was sold in favour of 68 Brook Street, a large, fashionable town house in Mayfair, leased in 1836 from the Grosvenors. Lady Anne's great uncle, William Pitt, was amongst the list of previous tenants of the property which, with the adjoining 66 Brook Street, now forms part of the Grosvenor Estate headquarters. It is interesting to note that 66 Brook Street underwent major changes in 1778, under the direction of none other than Samuel Wyatt who later designed Delamere Lodge.

Lady Anne was extremely fond of 68 Brook Street and continued to lease the property throughout the rest of her life. Certainly never one to hold back from the Wilbrahams' fortune she fitted the apartment with the most expensive furnishings and decor and for many years held court and entertained liberally here. One illuminating report of 1841 declares:

"Lady Anne Wilbraham has held 'a soiree dansante' at the family mansion

	Acres	r	p	Annual Rental Income		
				£	s	d
CUDDINGTON	512	3	1	1042	13	11
CROWTON	312	3	32	489	7	11
WEAVERHAM				13	2	0
BETCHTON	952	3	10	1671	19	2
WEEVER	1060	3	24	1562	3	6
CLIVE	231	1	5	360	3	9
MOSTON,TETTON	131	0	9	180	11	8
HUXLEY	252	1	31	300	0	0
NORLEY	4	1	25	12	0	0
STATHAM	1	0	36	3	0	0
OAKMERE	393	2	7	395	2	9
NANTWICH	74	2	5	398	7	2
WOOLSTON WOOD				19	0	0
HENHALL	77	1	9	172	10	0
CHIEF RENTS						
Arising from different Tenements				1	14	7
Total holding:	3927	2	18	6606	15	6

From the 1814 Marriage Settlement. George Wilbraham was, indeed, a wealthy man.

in Lower Brook Street at which over 200 of the leading fashionables in town honoured her Ladyship with their company, as also the chief members of the corps diplomatique."

This was Lady Anne at her best and, though it was certainly not her swansong in London society, the "soiree dansante" marked the conclusion of her husband's career at Westminster. The Wilbrahams could now turn their full attention to Delamere and a seismic change in their lives. London would remain an infrequent attraction but their future lay in Cheshire as a gentry family with George established as a country gentleman, magistrate, secretary of the Tarporley Hunt Club, High Sheriff and deeply involved in all manner of local and rural administrative duties. For her part, Lady Anne slipped effortlessly into her role as hostess to the county's leading luminaries. She also became much-respected for her work in the community, helping the needy and sick, establish-

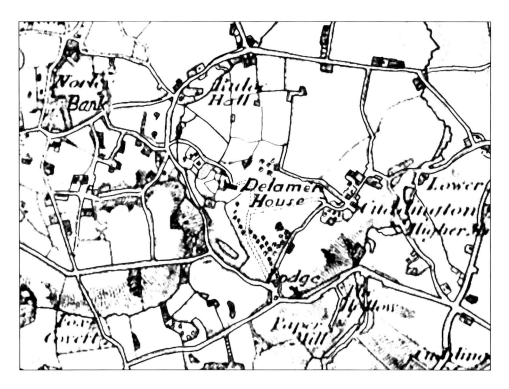

Greatly expanded from the 1842 Ordnance Survey Map, this is the first evidence of the lodge and, from it, the realigned drive to Delamere House and Lewis Wyatt's North-facing entrance.

ing a school at the Home Farm for the children of Wilbraham employees, and setting up a provident dispensary, in Weaverham, for the purpose of providing medical assistance to the labouring classes.

Lady Anne had prepared well for her permanent return to Cheshire and long before her husband stood down from Parliament she had drawn up grandiose plans to revitalise Delamere, to stamp it with the imprint of the noble Fortescues, a mansion appropriate and fitting to portray the Wilbrahams as perceived lords of Delamere Forest. The Ordnance Survey Maps of 1842 (the first produced) and 1873 reveal the extent of some of these plans and what appears to be a continuous programme spanning both George and Lady Anne's time, as well as during the tenure of their son, George Fortescue Wilbraham. The major changes in the 1820s are attributable to the designs of Lewis Wyatt (1777–1853), a nephew of Samuel Wyatt, who specialised in restyling hunting lodges into country mansions. He notably worked on Tatton from about 1807 and other commissions over the following twenty years included Kedleston Hall, Rode Hall, Heaton Hall, Oulton Hall and Plas Newydd.

The most salient external additions to Delamere Lodge included a stately new entrance, to the North East corner; construction of two towers on opposite sides of the West Wing; and a lean-to conservatory on the side of the dining room. The new entrance incorporated granite pillars and a flight of five steps over which was a canopied roof crowned by a wolf's head, the family symbol of the Wilbrahams. The original East door was replaced with a window and the former entrance made into an ante-room, or boudoir. Construction of the lean-to conservatory and the octagonal towers also provided alternative outlets to the newly-created formal gardens.

From the original open pastureland, approximately one-hundred acres of sweeping parkland was enclosed within a wrought-iron Cheshire fence, parts of which still exist in places and which has marked the perimeter of Delamere Park both as a military camp and the modern estate. Meanwhile, the whole of the immediate house grounds, including the stables, lawns, gardens and orchards, were separately enclosed and accessed via an elaborate gate.

A formal walled garden replaced the 200 square-feet conservatory and the

Delamere House, early 20th century, with the South Drive cutting through rolling parkland. This view is looking north west, from approximately the site of the Delamere Park tennis courts.

The South Drive passed alongside the modern tennis courts and curved towards Delamere House, now the setting for Westrees.

original coach-house was also removed, along with the former exercise paddock which became a smaller, walled garden with roses and fruit trees, through which ran a pathway leading to a summer house above Woods Lane.

Everything was on a grand scale, enhanced by the addition of the South Gate Lodge, a realigned South Drive and clever exposure of mature trees and new plantations in order to accentuate the "Delamere Forest" setting. To further emphasise its new status, "Delamere Lodge" was retitled "Delamere House", or perhaps "Delamere Hall", though in keeping with the tradition of other Cheshire family seats, such as Oulton (the Grey-Egertons), Vale Royal (the Cholmondeleys), Marbury (the Smith-Barrys), Eaton (the Grosvenors), Tatton (the Egertons), it simply became known as "Delamere". Wilbraham Diary entries all refer to "Delamere", never "Delamere Lodge" or "Delamere House"; villagers and staff knew it as "The Hall". It may be significant that the name change seems to have occurred about the time of the "Crown Land" enclosure of Delamere Forest and the creation, alongside the Chester highway at Oakmere, of one of the first new farms, "Delamere Lodge", suggesting the Wilbrahams' stately pile had already been retitled prior to the 1820s. This was the commencement of the true halcyon days at Delamere, when Delamere House shimmered, a shining symbol throughout the area, with its large retinue of retainers, estate workers and tenant farmers, its society gatherings and the family's munificence.

The following entry is contained in the "Mansions of England and Wales", published in 1850, and no doubt Lady Anne heartily approved of the description: "A handsome structure of stone in the modern style, it is pleasantly situated and surrounded with rich and extensive plantations (of about 100 acres). It contains a choice collection of paintings. The conservatories and gardens are on a large scale and display considerable taste in arrangement."

Bagshaws Directory, also published in 1850, went further, though the original title had stuck: "Delamere Lodge is an elegant modern mansion in a singular romantic situation built after a design by Wyatt. It is surrounded by a park, finely wooded and richly adorned with picturesque beauty".

As to the internal rearrangements, these too were extensive and, as it turned out, they were critical to the long-term stability of Delamere House. It is difficult to piece together the picture almost two centuries later, so a reliance has to be placed upon map comparisons and, to a degree, upon accounts from 20th century servants. The maps indicate large extensions to both the north-western and south-eastern corners of the house; one to provide a new kitchen, or utility, area and the other to form a two-storey servants' quarters. The purpose seems to have been to open up part of the West Wing in order to create a ballroom, a reconstruction that may have entailed the removal of several supporting walls, a pattern repeated in the construction of the grand new entrance hall. An innovation at Delamere, unconnected with either of the Wyatts, was the introduction, possibly during George Fortescue Wilbraham's era, of a heavy, lead water tank into the roof space of the West Wing. The water came from an extended pond on Small Brook, alongside Woods Lane, and was delivered, via hydraulic ram,

After ascending the front steps this was the view into the new Main Hall with its large Ionic columns. Left are the tubular bells at the foot of the staircase. The door to the right previously accessed the original entrance hall, part of which was converted into a Boudoir during Lewis Wyatt's alterations.

The last remains of the ice-house in Hunt's Hill Wood. George Fortescue Wilbraham planted the wood to provide for timber for the estate, though neither he nor his successors ever used it. Instead Hunt's Hill Wood became a favourite covert during the fox-hunting season and, with its abundance of pheasant and partridge, a venue for Delamere House shooting parties.

to a holding tank in the Delamere House lawn, from where it was hand-pumped, daily, to the roof. The pond has long silted up and now lies beneath a tangle of rhododendrons in Hunt's Hill Wood, though parts of the sandstone waterfall for the hydraulic ram are still evident, as is the nearby domed top of an ice-house which probably dates from the same period.

The weight of the water tank, the removal of supporting walls and pillars to facilitate Lady Anne's conversion, the soft-brick construction of the West Wing, and perhaps even Samuel Wyatt's design, undoubtedly contributed to a dilemma encountered by later Wilbrahams... the alarming condition of the Delamere House roof!

Early 20th century, showing household staff outside the Lewis Wyatt entrance. The granite pillars and flight of five steps are prominent and the different materials used in the original construction of Delamere Lodge can clearly be seen. To the left are the Exmoor granite blocks of the main house, whilst to the right are the bricks of the West Wing.

The corner of Delamere House West Wing showing the Pavilion, dating from the Samuel Wyatt design, and the servants' quarters, probably added by Lady Anne on the site of the Orangery. The Pavilion, fully glazed until the early years of the 20th century, seems to have been demolished during the 1920s. The door in the centre of the photograph originally led into the 200 square-feet conservatory.

To Earn a Sixpence !

GEORGE Wilbraham died in 1852, leaving Lady Anne and five sons, George Fortescue, Roger William, Thomas Edward, Henry and Hugh. The final part of his life is summarised in the Wilbraham Diary by George Fortescue:

> My Father died at Delamere, January 24, 1852, greatly regretted by all who knew him, leaving behind him the highest possible character for integrity and kindness in all the relations of his life. The latter years of his life, after his retirement from Parliament, were chiefly devoted to the ordinary duties of a country gentleman, to agriculture and management of his estates. The family vault at Nantwich, being closed by order of the Board of Health, I constructed a new vault in Weaverham Church Yard with the permission of the Vicar, the Rev. Charles Spencer Stanhope, and was then enabled to lay my Father's remains amongst those who best knew him and most highly valued him. His wife, Lady Anne is now living and in good health – October 1853.

When George Fortescue Wilbraham, unmarried and in the midst of forging a distinguished legal career in London, inherited at the age of thirty-seven, it was Lady Anne, "Her Ladyship" to most everyone, who continued to rule at Delamere House. Absent for a great deal of the time following his father's demise, George Fortescue was no doubt willing and compliant as his mother pressed on with her grand plans to revitalise the house and parkland. Later, and more so after Lady Anne's death, in 1864, he concentrated his own attention on the Cheshire estates, principally Delamere, and throughout the remainder of his lifetime pursued a sustained programme of improvement and expansion. Records of the 1870s show, precisely, his total acreage: 3,997 acres, 3 roods & 13 perches, with an estimated annual rent value of £7,948.

George Fortescue Wilbraham who redeveloped much of the Delamere House estate. He was, like his ancestors, greatly respected throughout Cheshire, a sentiment endorsed by James Hall's dedication in his "History of the Town & Parish of Nantwich" (1883): "To George Fortescue Wilbraham Esquire, of Delamere House, Cheshire, and to the Memory of his Ancestors who were long resident in the Town of Nantwich, and were the never-failing Guardians of its rights in by-gone days..."

Much of the existing estate was rebuilt, or extensively refurbished, during George Fortescue Wilbraham's custodianship, including the farmhouses of Cuddington Hall Farm and Poplar Farm. New dwellings included Poplar Cottages, Cuddington Bank Cottages, Gamekeeper's Cottage, Gardener's Cottage, the Home Farm Bailiff's Cottage, and North Lodge. The North Lodge and the North Drive may have been constructed to afford George Fortescue easier access to Acton Bridge Station and the railway to London.

The move towards smaller farms had a primary objective, to increase overall income from the Delamere House Estate. His parents' extravagances and the refurbishment of Delamere House had taken a demanding toll on the Robartes' money and George Fortescue, perhaps through necessity, was the first head of the Wilbrahams, of Townsend and Delamere, to be engaged in full-time employment, though it is more likely he, and certainly his mother, viewed the law as a calling rather than a profession.

On the subject of employment, one amusing anecdote recounts an occasion when, whilst walking back to Delamere House from the station at Cuddington, George Fortescue chanced upon three of his men building a beanstack. The evening was growing dusk and the men, wishing to finish the work before dark, called on the passer-by to help them, promising sixpence upon completion of the bargain. George Fortescue removed his coat and set to his task and when the stack was finished he asked for his money, the men by then realising exactly whom they had engaged. On getting back to Delamere House, he went straight to the housekeeper's room and threw his sixpence on the table. "There," he said. "That's the first sixpence I ever earned!".

Born at Delamere in 1815, George Fortescue was educated at Harrow and, like his father and grandfather, attended Trinity College, Cambridge. Following graduation he joined Lincoln's Inn and was called to the Bar in 1843, later serving for many years as a Home Circuit barrister based in London. In sharp contrast to his later passion for farming, which was perhaps a trait inherited from his grandfather, George Fortescue was a cultured man with fine taste who was responsible for establishing Delamere House's extensive library and rare works of art. Many of the portraits, certainly a Rembrandt, a Salvator Rosa and, possibly, a Titian, were collected by Lady Anne and transferred from the Brook Street, London house when the lease expired on the property in 1873.

Yewtree Cottage dates from 1706 and is the oldest surviving dwelling in Cuddington village. Originally Yewtree Farm, it became part of the Delamere House Estate around the turn of the 19th century. From the early 1900s, this photograph shows estate worker Roger Atherton and his daughter Eleanor who later became the wife of William Garner, the Cuddington butcher who served his apprenticeship working for the Wilbrahams at Home Farm.

Built in George Fortescue Wilbraham's time: Ruloe House, Gardener's Cottage and North Lodge. Near to Ruloe House is Summerhill, another former Wilbraham property.

In Cheshire, whilst engaged in his legal career, George Fortescue relied heavily upon his Agent to run the day-to-day management of the estates and, to accommodate this most senior representative of the family, he commissioned the celebrated Cheshire architect, John Douglas, a native of Sandiway, to build Ruloe House on a site acquired from the Smith Barrys. Douglas is also believed to have designed Overdale (1875), a many-chimneyed dwelling on the Tarporley Road, Oakmere which came to be the home of Henry, George Fortescue's brother. In the Wilbraham Diary, 1853, George Fortescue notes of his brothers:

> Roger William, obtained some years since a situation in Her Majesty's Treasury which he still holds. He married in September 1850, Louisa, daughter of Robert Gosling Esq. of Botleys Park, Surrey. Thomas Edward entered the Army in 1839 and rose to the rank of Captain but has lately retired. Henry took his degree of BA in 1846 at Trinity College, Cambridge, where he afterwards obtained a Fellowship – he is now practising as a Conveyancer at Lincoln's Inn. Hugh, having studied Agriculture, rents a farm in County Mayo and has also purchased some land in the same county.

Dating from 1868 this is the earliest known photograph of Delamere House. It shows the south east corner, with the granite-constructed main house and the West Wing. The lean-to conservatory and the octagonal tower were probably additions by Lady Anne. The Pavilion is visible at the far end of the lawn.

The huge expense incurred by George Fortescue in redeveloping the Delamere House estate was marred by two totally unexpected and costly occurrences. The first, during the 1850s, saw him spending £3,000 on major repairs to Delamere House, probably to the roof. The second, and more devastating, was in 1865 and related to a severe outbreak of rhinderpest amongst his cattle. George Fortescue states in the Wilbraham Diary:

> Towards the end of this year the County was visited by a severe pestilence among the cattle which continued to make terrible ravages throughout the following Spring and summer and could hardly be said to be extinct till November of this year, 1866. Many farms lost their entire stock, My own estates at Weaver, Huxley and Bechton were among the heaviest sufferers.

Despite these setbacks, the Delamere House Estate (now retitled the "Wilbraham Estate") continued to expand and flourish under George Fortescue, but he was certainly rationalising and finances were raised from the sale, to Wilbraham Tollemache, of most of his remaining lands in South Cheshire, and his very last transaction, shortly before his death in 1885, was to purchase "Ravenhead Farm" (Manor Farm), Cuddington, from the Smith Barrys.

The estate employed scores of outside workers and the 1861 Census lists the following ancillary staff at Home Farm: bailiff, butcher & assistant, schoolteacher, laundry woman. The domestic staff at Delamere House included a housekeeper, two housemaids, kitchenmaid, dairymaid, butler, footman, groom, gardener, gatehouse-keeper. Ten years later, the 1871 Census records thirty domestic servants, an indication of George Fortescue's lavish lifestyle during his latter years. Village fetes, garden parties and hunt balls were, under his venerable patronage, all part of the "Delamere" social scene.

George Fortescue did his stints as Secretary of the Tarporley Hunt Club and High Sheriff of Cheshire; he was also a local magistrate and, in 1881, joined with other Northwich and Winsford landowners to petition Parliament for a compensation bill to reimburse those whose properties were suffering from subsidence caused by brine pumping. They were unsuccessful, but ten years later the Brine Pumping Compensation Act did enter onto the Statute Book.

George Fortescue Wilbraham's death occurred at Delamere House on April 27, 1885 when he was succeeded by his brother, two years younger, Roger William Wilbraham who notes:

> George Fortescue Wilbraham was buried at Weaverham church in the family vault which was constructed by him. The coffins at this date (September 1885) in the vault are those of my father, of my mother, Lady Anne, who died February 1864, and also of my brother, Thomas Edward who died at Delamere House, November 1884. The principal events in the life of my brother have been noted by him. He was of a very quiet and unostentatious disposition, was well read in Classic and Literature, indeed much more so than was generally known. He took a considerable interest in the pictures, very many of which were cleaned and restored by Mr Barker, apparently with great judgement and care. It was during his life that the lease of the family residence in London, in Brook Street, fell in and he removed all the pictures, including the Rembrandt, to Delamere and arranged them in the Drawing Room.

George Fortescue's proud legacy was the Delamere House estate which he had expanded and refashioned into one of the most modern and efficient in Cheshire. Cuddington and Crowton were charming rural textbook villages with well-maintained farms and cottages and a loyal workforce, all dependent, in one way or another, upon the Wilbrahams. However, for many reasons, this pastoral idyll, which must have appeared timeless at George Fortescue's passing, was to be shattered in the lifetime of his great nephew. Wars and cataclysmic shifts in society values were contributory factors, but more than anything, the Robartes' money had been exhausted and the upkeep and repair of Delamere House was becoming something of a poisoned chalice.

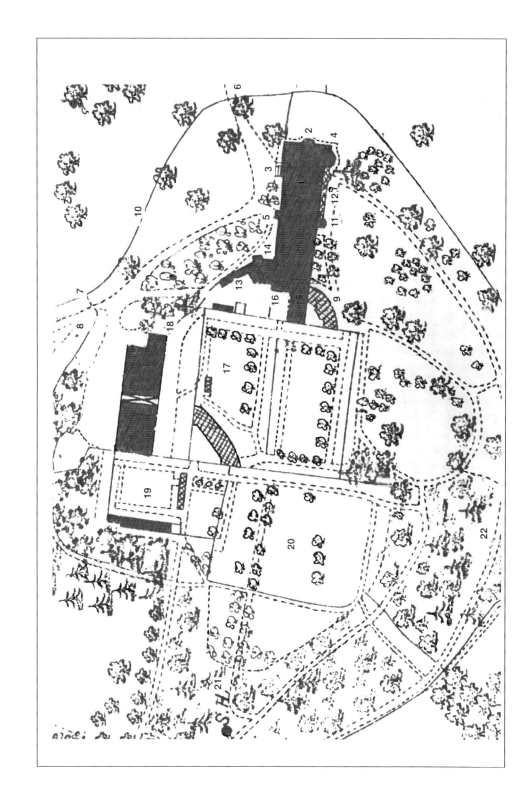

This enlarged extract from the Ordnance Survey Map of 1873 reveals many of the changes made to Delamere House by, principally, Lady Anne. The most noticeable of these is the new entrance (3), the addition of the towers on either side of the West Wing (5 & 11), and the large extension (14) to provide a new domestic kitchen complex. The full key is as follows:

1. Delamere House
2. The East front door has been abandoned and changed into a window.
3. A new pillared, grand entrance has been created on the North side, between the granite and brick construction.
4. A path has been laid around the East end of the house.
5. The North tower has been added.
6. The main drive has been realigned to sweep around the East valley contours and through an elaborate wrought-iron gate to the new entrance.
7. North Drive has been created. The original drive is now the "South Drive".
8. The original "South Drive", outside the formal gardens.
9. The Pavilion.
10. The whole of the House, stables, lawns and orchards enclosed within a wrought-iron "Cheshire fence".
11. The "Octagonal Tower", on the South side, has been constructed as an attractive outlet from the drawing room to the lawns and garden.
12. A cast-iron lean-to conservatory has been built from the "Octagonal Tower" to the granite front of the house. This extended over the Drawing Room windows to enhance the change from hunting lodge to Victorian mansion.
13. Original Orangery area replaced by a kitchen yard.
14. The North Western corner of the House has been extended, to accommodate a new domestic kitchen complex.
15. The South Western corner extended to form two-storey servants' quarters.
16. Samuel Wyatt's great corridor, from the House and through the Orangery to the Conservatory, has been abandoned.
17. The 200 feet-square Conservatory has been changed into a formal garden.
18. Coach-house and stableyard have been altered.
19. The Kennels and exercise yard absorbed into the garden area, possibly including cold frames, propagation areas and ancillary buildings.
20. The Victorian Walled garden.
21. The Summer House. This does not appear on an Estate Map of 1871, so was probably a recent addition.
22. A path from the Conservatory garden ran directly to the Summer House and woodland paths converged here. General area of an Arboretum.

The farmhouse of Home Farm, extended in modern times.

Lady Anne's school-room, with cart sheds below, was a purpose-built extension to an existing barn and is now used for storage. Lady Anne also provided a house, alongside the farmyard, for the school mistress.

Marsh Lane Farm, Crowton, demolished and replaced circa 1970. Farmed by the Rutters, this is now the Wilbraham Estate's Holly Bush Farm.
(Supplied by the Rutter family)

Home Farm, late 1960s. The large T-shaped barn, since replaced by a modern farm structure, included a dairy, bakery and abbatoir, all employed full-time until the end of the 19th century in the preparation of home-produced food for the Wilbrahams. The Home Farm, erected a suitable distance from Delamere Lodge to keep the farmyard smells away from aristocratic noses, was the vital cog in the efficient working of the estate, a model farm with cattle stores, carthorse stables, store-rooms, poultry houses, cart sheds etc... everything required to ensure the self-sufficiency of the Wilbrahams. Still part of the Wilbraham Estate, Home Farm has been tenanted by the Wheeldon family since the 1940s.
(Supplied by the Wheeldon family)

Six estate workers and their families lived at Cuddington Bank Cottages. The front three now form the single dwelling known as "Barrawitch", a corruption of "Barrastitch" which, in turn, is probably a corruption of "Barry's Ditch" which still carries the aquifer overflow from the edge of the "Townfields" to Cuddington Brook.

Cuddington Hall Farm, originally Firs Farm. Its renaming reflected the Fortescue Wilbraham's transformation of Delamere Lodge into a hall. The present farmhouse dates from 1874. Hall Farm has long been associated with the Kinsey family and remains part of the Wilbraham Estate.

Crowton Hall Farm, by far the oldest of the Wilbraham Estate farms, stands on the site of the moated Crowton Hall of the Normans and, possibly, the Saxons. The oldest part of the house can be seen at the rear of the main facade which appears to have been a Victorian addition, or rebuild. For many generations, Crowton Hall has been farmed by the Stubbs family.

The farmhouse to Poplar Farm (above) and Poplar Cottages (below left), in Cuddington Lane, date from George Fortescue Wilbraham. Farmed by the Clarkson family, Poplar Farm is still owned by the Wilbraham Estate.

Below is Top Farm, now a private dwelling. Other Wilbraham farms included Gallowsclough Lane Farm, Manor Farm, Watermill Farm and Camomile Farm.

Keepers Cottage, erected in 1871 by George Fortescue Wilbraham. His initials and the date are above the gable window. This was the home of successive Delamere House Estate gamekeepers. Game birds were reared in pens across the lane in Hunt's Hill Wood.

Another former Wilbraham property, The Mount, photographed about 1980. (Supplied by Ernie & Sue Elwell)

Titian's Lady, a heavy price to pay!

THE furniture, fittings and effects of Delamere House changed little from George Fortescue Wilbraham's 19th century tenure until its final closure in 1939, an event marked by a three-day auction sale organised to dispose of hundreds of items, ranging from simple kitchen utensils to volumes of rare books and valuable paintings. The accompanying catalogue, with a room-by-room inventory of lots, is the only surviving documentary evidence to reveal anything of the overall interior of the house.

The groundfloor included the following: Main Hall, Boudoir, Drawing Room, Dining Room, Library, Ante Room, Study, Ballroom, Servants' Hall, Little Room, Housekeeper's Room, Butler's Pantry, Kitchen and Lamp Room. Central to the groundfloor layout was a great oak-panelled corridor which, as we know, ran along the entire length of the spine of the West Wing. One

Delamere House in all its glory, around the turn of the 20th century.

Wilbraham servant of the early 20th century described this corridor as "large enough to drive a carriage down", obviously an exaggeration, but it was certainly wide. As to its length, this may be estimated from the sale catalogue's description of a "fitted Axminster runner", in two lengths, totalling approximately forty yards.

On the upper floor there were twenty-one bedrooms; twelve for the family and guests and nine for the servants, in the "far wing" and the "middle wing". There was also a Dressing Room, known as the "Yellow Room", a Bathroom, Lady's Maid's Room, and Night Nursery. As to the exterior descriptions, these refer to a large Motor House "under the Clock Tower", Conservatory, Stable Yard, First Garden, Second Garden, Small Yard, Rose Garden and the Summer House.

At the height of its pomp, particularly in the days of George Fortescue Wilbraham, Delamere House was adorned with the paintings he had collected, many by grand masters, and though these do not appear in the sale catalogue, the "Mansions of England and Wales" (1850) gives a list: Venus and Adonis, by Poussin; Christ Crowned with Thorns, by Corregio; Jew Rabbi, by Rembrandt;

The building of South Lodge and the new South Drive occurred during Lady Anne's changes. This evocative photograph, circa 1910, shows the lodge-keeper's wife, appropriately-named Mrs Lockett.

Roger Wilbraham and his wife Louisa

Magdalen, by Guercio; Landscape, by Swanfeldt; Lord Delamere and Lady Radnor, by Sir Peter Lely, and the most priceless of them all, Portrait of a Lady, by Titian. Hall's "History of Nantwich", published thirty-three years later, adds some of the family portraits at Delamere: Roger Wilbraham, of Nantwich, 1741, by Fellowes; Roger Wilbraham, of Dorfold, by Van Dyke; George Wilbraham, of Nantwich, by Battoni; George Wilbraham MP, by Jan Sheen; George Fortescue Wilbraham, by Williams Hall.

This then, with over three thousand acres of land, was Roger Wilbraham's inheritance when his bachelor brother died in 1885. Roger was sixty-seven and living in Hastings with his wife, Louisa Gosling, and the youngest of their nine children. His eldest son and heir, Arthur George Wilbraham is listed in the 1881 Census as being resident at the Raglan Barracks, in Devon, a lieutenant in the 1/13 Prince Albert's Somerset Light Infantry. Arth ur's younger brother, Sandhurst-trained Hugh Edward Wilbraham, is recorded as a lieutenant in the 82nd (South Lancashire) Regiment, stationed at North Camp, Farnborough, in Hampshire.

Later promoted to captain with the Somerset 2nd Battalion, Arthur George Wilbraham was probably nearing the end of his military career when, just at the moment of his uncle George Fortescue's death, Britain embarked upon what became known as the Third Burmese War (1885-87), to integrate Burma into the

The death of Arthur George Wilbraham was to have a profound effect on the long-term future of Delamere House. This photograph, early 20th century, further emphasises the brick construction of the West Wing, to the left.

British Empire and gain control of the country's raw materials. The Somerset 2nd Battalion was at the forefront of the fighting and, in July 1886, at the age of thirty, Captain Arthur George Wilbraham was killed in action. Roger Wilbraham records in the Wilbraham Diary:

> I received a telegram from India that my dear and eldest son, Arthur George, died on the 21st of July of wounds received in an attack made upon Dacoits in the Burma War. I will not here attempt to express my grief for his loss. He was educated at Harrow and was a fine Latin and Greek scholar.

It was the British Army's rule, until recent times, to bury the war dead in the country where they fell, so Captain Wilbraham, who should have inherited "Delamere", lies somewhere in Burma. His father erected a memorial plaque in St Mary's Church, Weaverham, and his name is listed on the Burma War Memorial, Taunton, which marks 144 members of the Somersets who perished in the conflict.

His father, Roger Wilbraham, had been born in 1817 and, educated at Harrow, spent the first year of an administrative career in a Liverpool Merchant's Counting House. Later he accepted a clerkship in the War Office, London, due, he says in the Wilbraham Diary, to the recommendation of Lord Stanley, of Alderley, who owned Winnington Hall, but also, no doubt, through the influence of his parents, Lady Anne and George who was by then a senior Member of Parliament.

In those days, a career in the Civil Service was exclusive to the upper classes, those whom a Parliamentary report dismissively described as "well-mannered, partridge-shooting fools... the sons of high aristocracy who have been accustomed to employ the Service as a means of providing for the waifs and strays of their families". Roger Wilbraham was nobody's fool and proved to be an extremely capable and conscientious civil servant who moved from the War Office to the Treasury where, over many years, he became Private Secretary to a succession of leading politicians, notably to the then Chancellor of the Exchequer, William Ewart Gladstone who was to become one of the iconic Prime Ministers of the Victorian era. Roger Wilbraham was Gladstone's Private Secretary at the time of the Crimean War when the great man was severely criticised for ill-equipping British troops. The following note from Gladstone, dated March 1854, may be alluding to this:

> My Dear Wilbraham
> Please to write letters according to the direction in Maude (Erskine-May) but you had better perhaps not have the item coppied out, and in any case send off nothing untill you have seen Sir A. Spearman who will arrange with you any points that may require clearance.
> Gladstone

The tragedy of Arthur George's death greatly affected Roger Wilbraham and though he was a much-respected village "squire" and magistrate, he was neither moderniser nor reformer, more a custodian of Delamere House and the Wilbraham-Fortescue legacy. Soon after Arthur George's death, Roger's second son, the new heir, Hugh Edward Wilbraham, retired from the army and established his home at Massey's Lodge, on the Tarporley Road, Oakmere. Here, in

From the Wilbrahams' Crowton Chapel in Weaverham St Mary's Parish Church.

The stained glass window and the marble memorial are to the memory of George Wilbraham MP (1779-1852) whilst the Hatchment, with Wolf's head, depicts the Wilbraham-Fortescue union.

The dedication (below) is to Lady Anne who died in 1864. All were erected by George Fortescue Wilbraham. The Wilbrahams have worshipped at Weaverham since the 18th century and the chapel contains numerous brass memorials to other members of the family.

Left, near to the church door, is the Wilbraham tomb, with the Wolf's head.

IN MEMORY OF LADY ANNE WILBRAHAM DAUGHTER OF HUGH 1ST EARL FORTESCUE AND WIFE OF THE ABOVE-NAMED GEORGE WILBRAHAM ESQ BORN OCTOBER 3RD 1787 DIED FEBRUARY 28TH 1864 "O LORD MY STRENGTH AND MY REDEEMER"

1890, his wife, Lilla Jane, gave birth to their first son, George Hugh de Vernon Wilbraham and, four years later, to Ralph (pronounced Rafe) Venables Wilbraham who came to be known throughout the family as "Sim". There were also three daughters, Vera May, who married Philip Coney Swayne, of Bridgewater, Somerset; Rhoda Joan, who married Robert Cyril Dewhurst, a son of a wealthy Manchester cotton manufacturer; and Barbara Francesca, who married Henry Ernest Plant, of Montreal, Canada.

Hugh Edward Wilbraham succeeded his father, Roger, in 1897.

Grandfather Roger Wilbraham must have been delighted that the family line of succession had been assured and to celebrate the birth of George Hugh de Vernon, the heir presumptive, he planted a Cedar of Lebanon on the ancient mound of the Delamere House parkland. This, to all Delamere Park residents, is now the "Captain's Tree", a tangible reminder of the last Wilbraham to occupy Delamere House.

Roger Wilbraham, eighty years old and after suffering a long illness, died on January 20, 1897 and was buried in the Weaverham family vault. Louisa, his wife, survived him for a further four years but, as was the general rule amongst landed families, she eventually vacated Delamere in favour of the incoming lady of the house, Hugh Edward's wife, Lilla Jane. Louisa Wilbraham died at her new home, near to Slough, in 1901.

Upon his inheritance, Hugh Edward Wilbraham, by then a Major with the Volunteer Battalion of the Cheshire Regiment, was immediately confronted with having to resolve some of the serious structural defects that had plagued Delamere House for upwards of forty years. The last major repairs had been under George Fortescue and the old place had rather been allowed to stagnate during Roger Wilbraham's time. Unfortunately, the enormous expenditure of past generations, on remodelling Delamere House and refashioning the estates, had caught up and the Major was certainly short of liquid capital with which to fund the most urgent repairs, then estimated at £3,000.

It was true he owned over three thousand acres of land in Cheshire, but the rents from farms and property, though substantial, probably only covered the running costs of a large mansion employing upwards of thirty domestic staff and at least equal this number of estate workers. Worse, agriculture was in depression. George Fortescue Wilbraham's vision, a noble one in the context of farming's "golden age", of rich profits based upon expanded and modernised estates, had evaporated under the weight of rising imports of cheap foodstuffs. Consequently, the Major was forced to resort to selling off family possessions. His entry in the Wilbraham Diary reads:

> The house at Delamere being in bad repair I had the same put in thorough order at a cost of about £3,000; to defray the cost I sold a portion of the Library at Messrs Sotheby, Wilkinson & Hodges Sale Rooms in London, on the 20th & 21st June 1898, the sale after deducting expenses bringing in about £2700.

For the next twenty years the Major, apparently, managed to keep on top of the problems during which time the Wilbrahams of Delamere House, basked in Edwardian and Georgian grandeur as the family hosted house parties, banquets, balls and hunt dinners. A nine-hole golf course was created in the fields behind Home Farm and numerous house guests stayed for the popular horse-race meetings at Chester and Tarporley, in April and May. During the winter months, shooting parties often spanned several days, most of the sport being centred around Hunt's Hill Wood where the gamekeeper reared his pheasants. A favourite village event inaugurated by the Major, and thoroughly enjoyed by people from miles around, was the annual Delamere House fete, held on August Monday.

Like many of his predecessors, Major Wilbraham was a leading member of

The south elevation of the West Wing of Delamere House with Lilla Jane, Major Hugh Edward Wilbraham's wife, in 1901.

The north elevation of the West Wing. The three-sided tower seems to have been added during Lady Anne's alterations, possibly to accommodate the ballroom. The door next to the tower may have been the family's private entrance into the grounds.

Riding in the park, at the top of the South Drive, are Major Wilbraham's daughter, Vera, who was known in the family as "Vere", and Esmond Bethell (left), with Bill Robinson in attendance. When Delamere House was demolished the ornate gate, seen in the background, was acquired by the Wilbrahams' solicitor who erected it at his home, Faulkners Lodge, in Christleton, where it still survives.

The Wilbraham coach was a familiar sight in the district, especially on Sundays when the family attended worship at St Mary's Parish Church, Weaverham. The coachman is Bill "Raunger" Robinson who, following a hunting accident, had to wear a false ear to support his top hat.

the Tarporley Hunt Club and also a Justice of the Peace, an Alderman of Cheshire and Chairman, 1896-1928, of Cuddington Parish Council. For services to the public he was awarded the MBE.

"The Green Collars", by Gordon Fergusson, relates an amusing anecdote concerning the Major in his latter days as a magistrate at Oakmere Courthouse when, due to his portliness, he was known to his friends as "Wobbles". Before him was Lord Tollemache, of Peckforton Castle, a fellow member of the Tarporley Hunt Club, who was alleged to have been speeding in his motor car at the Abbey Arms crossroads:

"The Inspector gave his evidence followed by the Sergeant who made the mistake of adding: 'And what's more your Worship, the car was going that fast, it blew me 'elmet off!' 'Don't believe it,' growled old Wobbles, 'case dismissed!'. It was a hot day and after a while, as other cases were brought before him, Major Wilbraham dozed off. He was long overdue for retirement, but efforts to get him to do so had been in vain. The Clerk nudged him and said: 'The verdict, Your Worship, the verdict'. Old Wobbles came too with a start. 'Fined five pounds,' he declared. 'We must put a stop to this furious driving'. The only trouble was that by then the case he was hearing concerned a young woman who was trying to get a paternity order."

The latter years of Major Wilbraham's life were blighted by the recurring expense of maintaining Delamere House and matters reached a crisis in the mid-1920s when it became clear that wholesale repairs would be required to the roof of the building which, in places, was no longer watertight. The Major's solution was again to turn to the family's possessions and, on this occasion, obviously due to the enormity of costs involved, he decided to sell the Titian, "Portrait of a Lady", oil on canvas, dated 1555.

How long this master had been in the ownership of the Wilbrahams is unknown, but records show that, titled "Titian's Daughter", it was loaned by the family to the British Institution in 1829, i.e. during Lady Anne's time, and the possibility arises that it came via the Robartes' inheritance and Uncle George Hunt's house in Upper Seymour Street, London. In 1883, the painting went on display, as "Caterina Coronaro", at the Royal Academy and, later, hung in the

The Wilbraham Titian, "Portrait of a Lady", 97.8 x 74 cm, now displayed in the National Gallery of Art, Washington DC. The view of the east end of the Delamere House Drawing Room shows the Titian mounted on the far wall.

drawing room of Delamere House. In 1927 it was sold by Major Wilbraham to the art dealers, Duveen Brothers, of New York, who, during the period 1909-1929, were engaged in transferring European art treasures, particularly paintings, to the mansions of America. The Samuel H. Kress Foundation purchased the Titian in 1938 and, in the following year, gifted it to the National Gallery of Art, in Washington DC, where it is now housed. The price paid by the Duveens to Major Wilbraham remains undisclosed, although the present family believes the sum to have been in the region of £10,000. The National Gallery of Art says the value of the "Portrait of a Lady" is now immeasurable!

Whatever the fee, subsequent events suggest it was never spent on the critical repairs to the Delamere House roof and nor, indeed, were the proceeds from a further two-day Sotheby's sale, in March, 1928, "A Selection from the Library of Delamere House" which included, as one of principal lots, a "fine copy" of Grey's Elegy, dated 1751. A copy of the sale catalogue survives in the archives of the Deering Library, at the Northwestern University, Nairobi, probably carried there by one of the colonials, possibly George Hugh de Vernon Wilbraham who, as we shall see later, spent a number of years in Kenya.

The Hunt meets on the lawns of Delamere House, circa 1905. Major Wilbraham's daughters view the gathering from the first floor windows. (Trevor Booth Collection)

Hugh Edward Wilbraham's wife Lilla Jane Coney, third right, with her mother and bridesmaids on her wedding day. Lilla Jane's father was the Rev. Thomas Coney, Chaplain to the Forces.

Above: Hugh Edward's mother, Louisa with members of her family in the 1890s. House guest Herbert Swayne is showing off a bite inflicted by his pet snake!

Left: On the steps of Delamere House, Hugh Edward's sisters, Alice, Beatrice and Ada.

Lilla Jane, with the children and their friends, outside the Pavilion, circa 1895. George Wilbraham, who was to demolish Delamere House, is on the see-saw.

A few years earlier, outside the stables. Hugh Edward is holding George.

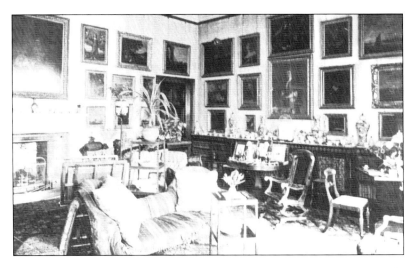

Delamere House Drawing Room adorned with valuable paintings. In the lower photograph, the Titian is seen on the right with, beneath it, a large ornate sideboard carved with George Fortescue Wilbraham's initials.

The Dining Room showing design features by different architects. The alcove is typical Samuel Wyatt, whilst the fireplace, similar to examples at Tatton, is Lewis Wyatt. From mid-Victorian times the Dining Room was dominated by an enormous sideboard which had, set within it, a towering, almost life-size portrait of George Fortescue Wilbraham. This can be seen on the left wall in the bottom photograph.

The Delamere House Library (here) and the Drawing Room contained thousands of books, many of them rare first editions. Some of these were sold through Sotheby's, but the majority were disposed of in the closing down sale in 1939. The Grecian urns on the bookcase were collected by George Wilbraham during his Grand Tour in the 18th century.

This circular room, the Upstairs' Boudoir, was at the front of the house, immediately beneath Samuel Wyatt's cupola. The double doors are still in the possession of the Wilbraham family.

A family gathering in 1901 outside the West Wing. Rhoda, Mrs Bethell, Lilla Jane, Hugh Edward, Barbara and, playing with the dogs, George. The door here may have been at the end of the great corridor and led into the walled garden.

Bill "Raunger" Robinson with Lilla Jane and baby Ralph at Delamere House in 1895. This was prior to the death of Roger Wilbraham and Lilla Jane and Ralph had probably driven over from Masseys Lodge.

The Delamere Forest ambience was accentuated with woodland paths, such as this one above Woods Lane. Right: Lilla Jane Wilbraham with two of her daughters, Rhoda and Barbara.

At the octagonal tower family entrance to Delamere House, circa 1910. Hugh Edward Wilbraham (left) with Philip Swayne, and almost certainly Joseph Charlton Parr and his son-in-law Robert Soame Jocelyn, the 8th Earl of Roden. Parr was the head of Parr's Bank (Warrington), one of the forerunners of the National Westminster Bank. Like Major Wilbraham, he was a Cheshire Alderman, Justice of the Peace and Chairman of Magistrates. Parr's daughter, Elinor Jesse Parr, was the Countess of Roden, the family seat being Tollymore Park, County Down.

Lilla Jane and daughter Rhoda enjoy the tranquility of the Victorian walled garden.

A group of Delamere House Estate staff in Major Wilbraham's time.
In the centre, holding his stick, is the Agent, George Garfitt.

It was not uncommon for members of the landed gentry to establish their own troops of militia comprised of estate workers and tenants. This is the Delamere House troop, circa 1910. Because the men were kitted out in second-hand uniforms, acquired by Major Wilbraham from the Cheshire Yeomanry, they were scoffingly referred to locally as "Wilbraham's Rag-arsed Militia".

The old cottages in Park Lane and another view of South Lodge.

Major Wilbraham was the first to own a motor-car in the village. Purchased in London it was delivered to Delamere House by the showroom salesmen who then had the task of teaching one of the Wilbraham grooms, here, to drive. In turn, the groom passed on his new-found skill to his colleagues. The nearest petrol station was in Northwich.

The Years of Reckoning

GEORGE Hugh de Vernon Wilbraham was a young man in a hurry when he left Harrow School in about 1908. By the following year he was big-game hunting in East Africa, in the company of P.K.Glazebrook who was later to become a Member of Parliament for South Manchester and a Major with the Cheshire Yeomanry. The 2,000-mile Mombasa-Nairobi railway had opened up Kenya to aristocratic British settlers headed by the 3rd Lord Delamere, Hugh Cholmondeley, of Vale Royal (Whitegate), and in Britain big-game hunters were being courted to board the "lunatic express" to adventure and excitement. George, at nineteen and in his element, was present when Glazebrook shot the "largest lion that had ever fallen to a gun of a modern sportsman".

Kenya's green valleys at the foot of Mount Kenya were developing into a playground for the rich and recalcitrant, the likes of Lord Egerton, of Tatton, and Lords Cranworth, Hindlip, Cardross, and Lord Delamere's brothers-in-law, the Coles, who were sons of the Earl of Enniskillen, of Sandiway. These were the aristocrats who turned the "White Highlands" into a Little England, with comfortable stone houses, panelled drawing rooms and morning glory bursting into bud around the verandas. As one writer put it, these were the "daffodil days of peacocks, champagne and sundowners, of horse racing, hunting and woman-ising". During the 1920s and 1930s, this was the notorious "Happy Valley" set whose antics coined the joke: "Are you married, or do you live in Kenya?"

George Wilbraham obviously found life exhilarating in Kenya and though he returned to England in February 1911, apparently to join the Cheshire Yeomanry as a 2nd Lieutenant, his homecoming coincided with his twenty-first birthday celebrations. However, by the time of his sister, Vera May's wedding, in September 1912, he was back in East Africa. A ball at Delamere marked his coming-of-age and estate workers and tenants enjoyed the family's ceremonial tapping of a barrel of beer, traditionally sealed at the birth of an heir and then stored for twenty-one years in the Delamere House wine cellars. The celebrations concluded with a huge bonfire and fireworks' display in the park.

Vera May Wilbraham's marriage to Philip Swayne, of Somerset, at the Church of St Peter's, in Cranley Gardens, London, was a society occasion of the highest order, one of the last ever to be associated with Delamere House. The press commented: "Although the wedding took place in London, the utmost interest was aroused in the event in all parts of Cheshire and this was only to be expected having regard to the fact that the bride belongs to one of the oldest and most highly respected families in the county." It w as noted that Mr Ralph Wilbraham officiated as groomsman "in the absence of his brother, Mr George Wilbraham who has recently gone to East Africa on a big-game hunting expedition".

Major Wilbraham's tenants presented the bride with an enamelled watch, set

Young George Wilbraham, with his man servant, Jack Yearsley, about to set off for big-game hunting in East Africa.

FASHIONABLE CHESHIRE WEDDINGS.

MISS VERA MAY WILBRAHAM MARRIED IN LONDON.

A BRILLIANT SCENE.

THE BRIDE.

THE BRIDEGROOM.

The wedding of Vera Wilbraham and Philip Swayne made the headlines in 1912.

with diamonds; the estate workers gave a silver salver and the household servants a china breakfast service. The press added: "Members of the household staff and head employees on the Delamere House estate were invited to inspect the presents on Friday afternoon and were afterwards entertained to a sumptuous tea in the hall. On Saturday afternoon the estate labourers and their wives were provided with a similar repast, and also had the opportunity of viewing the wedding gifts received by the bride."

At the outbreak of the First World War, in August 1914, and with Kenya a British protectorate, a rush of Empire volunteers rallied to the flag in Nairobi and irregular units of mounted horse were collectively formed into the East African Mounted Rifles, later absorbed into the 1/7 King's African Rifles (Kenya). Records show that George Wilbraham, resident in the country for the best part of six years, joined the irregulars as a private, but few, if any, shots were fired in anger and, either from of a sense of duty, or because pressed to do so, he set sail for England in 1915, to rejoin with the Cheshire Yeomanry. This was at a time prior to the introduction of conscription and his commanders were unimpressed with their erstwhile 2nd Lieutenant who must have been viewed in the same vein as Major Maurice Egerton (the future Lord Egerton of Tatton) who had spent the first eight months of the war also in Kenya. Maurice Egerton was refused permission to rejoin the Cheshires for, as the regimental history records: "A man so little interested in his country and regiment was no proper person to join even the 2nd Line.".

For his part, George Wilbraham was allowed in, but only as a humble officer in the 3rd Line, in charge of an equine remount depot in his own village of

Cuddington. Ironically at this time, his mother, Lilla Jane was said to be "rabble-rousing" the young men of the district to join the colours.

A dire shortage of manpower, particularly of officer class, subsequently led to George Wilbraham being promoted to the rank of Captain and, in December 1916, he was dispatched to the front line in Egypt. Remarkably, this was a sojourn that lasted for only a few weeks as, in February 1917, Captain Wilbraham was allowed to take his leave and return to Kenya and the 1/7 King's African Rifles, then engaged in a series of minor skirmishes and guerilla actions associated with the East African campaign.

Throughout the rest of his life, George always insisted upon being addressed as the "Captain", never Mr Wilbraham. Meanwhile, his brother, Ralph, a Brigade Signals Officer with the Cheshire Yeomanry, distinguished himself at the Battle of Beersheba, Palestine, and was awarded the Military Cross. He later fought with his regiment in France. George's friend, Major P.K.Glazebrook was killed in 1918 whilst serving with the King's Shropshire Light Infantry which

Officers of the Cheshire Yeomanry one week before embarkation for Egypt in 1915. 2nd Lieutenant Ralph Wilbraham is on the extreme right, back row, and Major Glazebrook, whom George Wilbraham had accompanied to East Africa, is on the front row, third left.

had merged with the Cheshires prior to the Palestine campaign.

Within weeks of the Armistice, Captain George Wilbraham resigned from the 1/7 King's African Rifles and returned to England to prepare for his wedding, in March 1919, to Kathleen "Kitty" Neilson, the eldest daughter of Henry Cottingham Neilson, of Plovers Moss, Oakmere. The ceremony took place at St Peter's Church, Delamere and the Northwich Guardian reported:

"The quaint little church was crowded with representatives of well known Cheshire county families on the occasion of the marriage of Captain G.H.Wilbraham, of the King's African Rifles. Captain Wilbraham, who was farming in British East Africa when the war broke out, was recalled to the Cheshire Imperial Yeomanry and for four months he was campaigning in Palestine and then, on his own request, was transferred to the King's African Rifles and remained fighting with them until the armistice was signed. The bridegroom, attired in khaki, was accompanied by the best man, Captain Peddar, also in officer's uniform." (This press information, "provided by the bridegroom", was misleading, to say the least. George had actually been no further than Egypt and prior to the Palestine campaign had left to return to Kenya.)

A reception was held at Plovers Moss and one month later, Captain Wilbraham and his bride departed for the "Happy Valley" set in Kenya where,

Plovers Moss, the home of Henry Cottingham Neilson whose daughter, Kathleen, married George Wilbraham in 1919.

throughout most of the 1920s, he was able to indulge his passions for horse-racing, shooting and gambling, and whatever else went with the territory.

All the while it was Major Hugh Wilbraham who carried the burden of Delamere House's deteriorating condition, a situation so desperate that he felt forced to sell the Titian and more of the library collection. George Wilbraham's role in the sales, during 1927 and 1928, are not clear, but the dates do seem to coincide with his return from Kenya when he and Kitty took up resi-dence at The Mount, an estate property, in Cuddington Lane. If George was entrusted by

Major Hugh Wilbraham was forced to sell the Titian to pay for the urgent repairs to Delamere House.

his ageing father with the responsibility of commissioning the repairs to the house, they never took place. The money was destined for other purposes.

Major Hugh Edward Wilbraham, a man of outstanding public service and undoubtedly the most respected of all the Wilbrahams who ever resided at Delamere House, died in May, 1930. The Bishop of Chester noted: "It would take pages of writing to describe all that he has done. He overtaxed his failing strength to visit his dying brother (Henry Dudley Wilbraham) in London; he came back to Delamere just to die. It is dreadfully sad to think of his dear home left sorrowing, Delamere, in its own way, so perfect."

At the time of his death Major Wilbraham was chairman of the following: Eddisbury Justices, the River Weaver Navigation Trustees, the Governors of Sir John Deane's Grammar School and the Northwich Education Authority. He was also President of the Northwich Victoria Infirmary, a former chairman of numerous other bodies, including both Cuddington and Crowton Parish Councils, secretary of the Tarporley Hunt Club and one of the foremost bene-factors of Weaverham Parish Church. The Northwich Guardian wrote of the funeral at Weaverham: "Almost every house and shop had its blinds drawn and the countryside for miles around showed signs of sympathy. As the cortege wended its way through the thickly-lined streets of the old-world village, the utmost reverence was shown. Leaders of public life assembled at the church from all parts of the county, together with agriculturists and others who had learned to admire the late Major for his sterling work. It might be said of him that he practically devoted the whole of his life to public service and he was a gentleman of the strictest integrity."

The pall bearers were eight county constables and at the entrance to the church gates were representatives of the Cheshire Hunt, in full scarlet attire. A motor-lorry was required to convey the floral tributes to Weaverham, from public bodies, as well as neighbours, tenants and staff. One, poignantly marking the family's centuries old links with Nantwich, was sent by the "Widows and Maids, Almshouses at Welsh Row, Nantwich".

Tributes were expressed throughout the county, for as the Rev E.S.Oliver, preaching at Witton Parish Church, remarked: "There are few departments of public service in the neighbourhood in which Major Wilbraham did not take an active, a valuable and conspicuous part. All that he did, he did so thoroughly, he did so quietly and unstintingly. There was no thirst for popularity, no evidence of selfish ambition."

J. Arthur Cowley, the Clerk of Northwich Urban Council, best summed up the Major's life in a letter to Lilla Jane: "Your husband has displayed a courage and made sacrifices in his public life which set an outstanding example to be followed by those who succeed him. He was not counted amongst those who make leisure and enjoyment the supreme contentment of life."

The Major had reigned at Delamere House for over thirty years and now it was the turn of the Captain. Unfortunately, George Wilbraham immediately faced a crisis never previously encountered by any of his forebears, i.e. estate duty, otherwise known as death duty, introduced in 1894 and rigorously tightened by the Chancellor of the Exchequer, Lloyd George, to such an extent that by the end of the First World War, members of the landed gentry everywhere were said to be in "full retreat". George Wilbraham, whether he had dipped into the Titian proceeds for personal use, or he had shrewdly set it aside for the consequences of his father's demise, was confronted with having to raise the staggering tax sum of £46,000 which, using the Bank of England's retail price index, is equivalent to £2 million. He blandly commented in the Wilbraham Diary:

> In 1932 I sold the Becheton (Sandbach) properties and the Wilbraham Arms, Nantwich, to pay £46,000 death duties.

Still a major landlord, with many tenanted farms and cottages, George was then dealt another severe blow, in 1934, when the local authorities of Northwich and Winsford ordered the modernisation of all habitable properties, essentially to incorporate inside lavatories and bathrooms. This time there was a more weary acceptance in George's Diary note:

> The Weaver and Delamere House estates being in such bad repair and being compelled by the councils concerned to bring all buildings up to date, I was compelled to part with the Weaver estate.

The latter was, of course, the 1,000-acre Weaver Hall estate, south of the River Weaver, near to Winsford, and its sale emphasises George Wilbraham's spiralling circumstances. It was by far the largest of the family's estates and the rents had yielded a significant income for two-hundred years. To make matters worse amidst this turmoil, George discovered that his wife, Kitty, was having an

LEGAL NOTICES.

I, GEORGE HUGH de VERNON WILBRAHAM, of Delamere House, Northwich, Cheshire, HEREBY GIVE NOTICE that I will NOT BE RESPONSIBLE for any DEBTS incurred or to be incurred by my wife lately of the same address and that she has not my authority to pledge my credit.
Dated this 17th day of July, 1935.
G. H. de V. WILBRAHAM.
Witness to the signature of the said George Hugh de Vernon Wilbraham :—
Jas. W. Lund, Secretary,
Cuddington Cottage,
Cuddington, Northwich.   123a

JESSE WILLIAMS, Deceased.

From the Northwich Guardian, July 1935, when George Wilbraham was making a very public show of separating from his first wife, Kathleen. By this time, Cuddington Cottage had become the estate office.

affair and, in a fit of outrage, he shot her dogs and then placed a public notice in the local press, declaring he would no longer be responsible for any debts incurred, or to be incurred, "… by my wife lately of the same address (Delamere House)". Kitty left the area with her lover and George, who had a reputation for his own extra-marital liaisons, successfully filed for divorce on the grounds of infidelity.

George continued to reside at Delamere House, but by the mid-1930s his roving eye had turned towards Roberta ("Bertha") Bullock, almost twenty years his junior. Bertha was the daughter of a famous ex-jockey William (Billy) Bullock, of Malton, Yorkshire, who had notably ridden a filly named Signorinetta to victory in the Oaks and Derby classics of 1908; in the latter race she was said to have won in a canter, at odds of 100-1. Following the First World War, Billy Bullock was the leading jockey in Denmark and here Bertha must have received part of her education. Later he was work jockey at the Malton stables of Captain

Portraits of George and Bertha, from their wedding in 1937.

Charles Elsey and this may have been where George Wilbraham, a racehorse owner himself, met his future wife.

George's mother certainly did not approve of him marrying a jockey's daughter, a far cry, indeed, from the unions of his ancestor into the Robartes' family fortune and the prestige associated with marriage into the Fortescues. On their wedding day, at Northwich Register Office, on October 14, 1937, George was forty-seven and showing his age, whilst Bertha, at twenty-eight, was an attractive young woman, in her prime. Remarkably, this somewhat mismatch of a marriage survived many troubled times until George's death in 1962.

Long before marriage to Bertha, George had been wrestling with the prob-

Wedding memories: With Ralph and Mary Wilbraham, Bertha Bullock about to leave Brook House for her marriage to George Wilbraham at Northwich Register Office. The lower photograph shows the happy couple setting off from Delamere House on their honeymoon. Bertha's mother is in the centre, standing alongside Ralph. To the left is Lilla Jane Wilbraham's long-serving companion, Miss Telford.

lem of what to do about Delamere House. In the years since the sale of the Titian its condition had steadily worsened, rather like the state of his finances, though in the early 1930s, with typical bluster, he outwardly appeared not to be too concerned about either. Iris (Hewitt) Pearson, a housemaid at Delamere House recalls:

"It was a fine place and there was a wonderful camaraderie amongst the staff. I lived in and worked for Captain Wilbraham and his wife, Kitty; his mother was there as well. We didn't get much time off, other than Sunday afternoons. Inside the house you could literally drive a horse and carriage along the passage from the kitchen to the hall. Everywhere was block floors and double doors and there was a ballroom off the hall; it was in black and white marble. The Captain and Mrs Wilbraham used to arrange balls attended by the likes of the Duke of Westminster and his daughters. They did an awful lot of entertaining, like Royalty, and they didn't seem short of money. When the balls were taking place all the chauffeurs would sit down to a meal in the enormous servants' hall. These were wonderful occasions."

George Wilbraham's marriage to Bertha brought an abrupt end to Delamere House, the family seat since 1784.

The old cottages on Park Lane, late 1920s, with Mrs Dutton and her grand-son, David Fahey who went on to work as a butler at Delamere House. The cottages were demolished during the war on the instructions of George Wilbraham. (David Dutton Collection)

Things were about to change, however, and the circumstances that led to the demise of Delamere House may not have been entirely due to its structural condition. Lilla Jane and Ralph Wilbraham proposed demolition of the "soft brick" West Wing, to leave the main granite building as a refurbished country house; a sensible idea which, had George remained with his first wife, might possibly have happened. Instead, Kitty's affair and his rebound marriage to Bertha Bullock changed the entire scenario and Lilla Jane and Ralph never forgave him. Bertha was vehemently opposed to living at Delamere House and George, whether indulging her, or simply determined to resolve what he perceived to be a financial millstone, decided to quit the place and build a new marital home, Delamere Manor, in a tranquil setting overlooking Cuddington Pool. George's entry in the Wilbraham Diary reads:

> Delamere House being too large for present state requirements and what with subsidences and other acts of God, I decided to build Delamere Manor which I entered on December 7th, 1938, furnishing it partly with all that was best out of Delamere House.

The 1930s was certainly a decade of reckoning for George Wilbraham. His

ADMIT BEARER TO PUBLIC VIEW AND SALE.

By direction of CAPTAIN G. H. WILBRAHAM.

Delamere House, Northwich,
CHESHIRE.

CATALOGUE

Of the Greater Portion of the

Contents of the Mansion

embracing

ENGLISH PERIOD FURNITURE .

CARPETS AND RUGS,

Appointments of Principal and Secondary Bedrooms

Early English and Oriental PORCELAIN and CHiNA.
100 Pewter Plates and Dishes.　　Copper and Brassware.

OIL PAINTINGS and ENGRAVINGS by eminent Artists.

A UNIQUE CIVIL WAR CHEST.

LIBRARY OF NEARLY 3000 VOLUMES

including many first & early editions, Bric-a-Brac, Miscellanea and other General Furnishings, including a nearly new Electrolux Refrigerator.

GARDEN AND OUTDOOR EFFECTS.

———————➤◇◠◠◝———————

HENRY MANLEY & SONS, LTD.

(R. Manley, F.A.I. and E. E. Wright, F.A.I.)

are instructed to Sell by Auction, on the Premises

On WEDNESDAY, 18th JANUARY, 1939,

AND TWO FOLLOWING DAYS, at 11-30 a.m. each day.

Catalogue, price 1/- each. obtainable from the Auctioneers' Offices, or the place of Sale on View Day.

Public View, Monday, 16th January, 1939, from 9-30 a.m. to 5-30 p.m. Admission to View and to Sale Room by Catalogue.

Auctioneers' Offices : Crewe [Telephone 2654], Whitchurch [Telephone 19], Nantwich and Market Drayton.

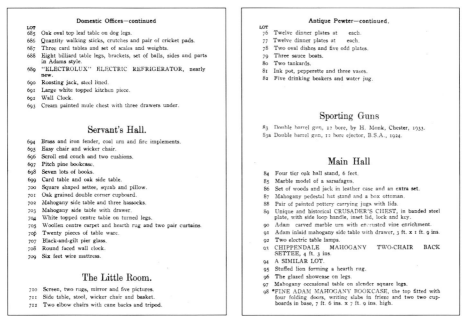

The sale spanned three days and attracted buyers and sightseers in hundreds. These pages from the sale catalogue give a small sample of the lots.

father had died leaving him with enormous death duties; he had been through the divorce courts, married Bertha Bullock, given up Delamere House, built Delamere Manor, and then, just as things seemed to be turning in his favour, came the outbreak of the Second World War to further undermine whatever plans he had in mind for the former Delamere House parkland.

Ignoring the protests of his family, George and Bertha seem to have proceeded on their course from the time of their honeymoon and Delamere Manor was designed and built in little over a year. A record does not exist of the costs incurred but these must have been substantial and one gets the impression that George was financially overstretching himself. With a few exceptions, and with George's mother, Lilla Jane, having moved away, the entire Delamere House workforce was dismissed in anticipation of the contents sale, the likes of which had never previously been witnessed in the district.

The sale took place in January, 1939, spanned three days and included just short of 1,200 lots and the 48-page catalogue, detailing an amazing range of items, clearly shows that George was out for every penny. Included alongside

George and Bertha's Delamere Manor, loosely modelled on Delamere House, without the West Wing. Delamere Manor overlooks Cuddington Pool (Ladypool) and stands alongside Cuddington Waste, held by the Wilbrahams under a "chief rent" of five shillings per year from the Smith Barrys, Lords of the Manor. Shortly before his death, in 1885, George Fortescue Wilbraham purchased Ravenhead Farm and when Delamere Manor was built it was renamed "Manor Farm".

Queen Anne chairs, furniture by Chippendale and Sheraton, Adam fireplaces, Axminster carpets and rare paintings, were twenty part-sets of knights' armour, walking sticks, chicken wire, fruit trees, plant pots, an Electrolux refrigerator, over 300 lots of books and a portfolio of ancestral family documents. Poignantly, one name stands out amongst the hundreds of successful bidders over the three days... Ralph Wilbraham, George's brother, who managed to purchase a medicine cupboard from his mother's bedroom and the doors from her Boudoir.

The interior sale complete, George, with ruthless efficiency, then set about selling off the entire fabric of Delamere House, including the Exmoor granite blocks, Samuel Wyatt's copper dome, slates, doors, window frames, skirting, panelling, garden gates, turf from the lawns and practically every item of masonry and timber from the stables and outbuildings. The Delamere House clock, whose chime had governed the lives of estate workers since the turn of the 19th century, was acquired by the Lockers, of Beechfield (now Lamb's Grange), and the demolished house bricks, originally fashioned from the clay of Cuddington Waste, were carted away to be used as hardcore in the construction of the Hartford-Sandiway section of Northwich bypass.

One of the large carpets, originally from Delamere House, receives a thorough spring-clean outside the Manor, with Mrs Howells, the cook, and maid, Dorothy Antrobus.

By the time it was over, only the foundations remained of George Wilbraham's hunting lodge, Lady Anne's high-society mansion, George Fortescue's pride and joy. It was a sad scene as villagers watched over the final ignominy, the felling of a row of stately trees, near to the North Drive, sold to the timber merchants, Littlers of Northwich. With astonishing haste, less than three months after moving into Delamere Manor, George Wilbraham had clinically erased Delamere House from the maps.

Lady-of-the-Manor: Bertha Wilbraham, circa 1940.

Left: The Delamere Manor gamekeeper, Tim Atkinson who lived in one of the cottages at the end of the drive. His father had also been a gamekeeper with the Wilbrahams. Right: With war declared, a local builder commences to fit blackouts to the windows of the Manor.

A staff break at Delamere Manor for (left to right) Winnie Hickson, Mrs Rowlands, Betty Buckley and Mrs Howells.

A holiday snap in Scotsberg during the 1930s. George Wilbraham (nearest camera) with his father-in-law, Billy Bullock, Bertha and her sister, Gretha. Billy Bullock had been the leading jockey in Denmark after the First World War.

Mrs McLewley, the cook and housekeeper of many years at Delamere House, outside the bungalow (next to Cuddington Bowling Club) which George Wilbraham had built for her retirement. The Bowling Club pays an annual rent of only five pence to rent the green from the Wilbraham Estate.

The Military 'Invasion'

THE once picturesque parkland of Delamere House had been abandoned to its fate for almost a year when Hitler's troops stormed into Poland and war erupted over Britain, in September 1939. Soon, land and property everywhere was commandeered for the "Home Front", controlled by Defence Regulations issued under the Emergency Powers (Defence) Act, and semi-derelict rural locations were particularly attractive for all manner of military purposes. In s ome instances, local authorities were encouraged to recommend sites to the War Department and George Wilbraham, a member of Cheshire County Council, would doubtless have supported requisition of Delamere House park. Compensation generally came at £60.00 an acre with a commitment that, at the end of the war, whenever that might be, the landowner would be able to buy back his land at the same fixed price.

Approximately sixty acres of the Delamere House parkland was commandeered and following an early survey, undertaken by the Royal Engineers, the site officially became "Delamere House Transit Camp", essentially sited around the South Lodge entrance and Park Lane. Nissen huts were erected and, initially, the camp housed recruitment facilities for the district. Then, during the months of the "Phoney War", a battery of Royal Artillery began to slip discreetly into position with their Anti-Aircraft (Ack Ack) guns, in readiness for the inevitable German bomber raids on Liverpool Docks and the ICI works at Runcorn. When the attacks became a reality, the 3.8-inch mobile guns were trundled around the country lanes on Matador heavy trucks and fired from natural sites around Cuddington, Crowton and Norley. Searchlights were dotted about the area, one being in Bent Lane, and overall operations were controlled from a command post, possibly sited in one of the fields off Park Lane.

A computer enhanced illustration from the photograph below of the Lodge entrance to the Royal Artillery Camp, in 1939/40. The Royal Artillery badge is in the foreground, in front of a Nissen hut that served as the guard room. The other Nissen huts were store sheds and barracks and to the left, behind the

trees, are the officers' accommodation huts. In the background, parked alongside the large Nissens, are the Matador trailers. The standing pillar is now incorporated into the Wilbraham Gate.

Raids were at their heaviest during the dark days of 1940. Bombs fell near to Cuddington Hall Farm and Bryn Smithy, and Nook Farm, Gorstage, alongside the London-Scotland mainline railway, was totally destroyed. One story is told of an unexploded landmine and a village lad dangerously cutting away the parachute which he promptly delivered to his mother who turned the material into cushion covers. In 1940 George Wilbraham wrote in his Diary:

> On the night of 28 November my village of Upper Cuddington was damaged by German bombs to the extent of £1,000 – my poor brother, Rafe was taken prisoner by the Germans on June 6th.

The United States did not enter the war until after Pearl Harbour, at the end of 1941, but for some time Britain had been in busy preparation and an architect, William A. Singleton, was commissioned to design two full-blown army camps at Oulton Hall and Delamere House. Years later Singleton wrote:

"Through the good offices of Captain G.H. Wilbraham, who owns Delamere Park Estate and who built Delamere Manor, I had the use of a cottage adjoining the Manor. Many memories of my happy stay in this part of Cheshire flood back into my mind, and several of them are memories of situations which could only

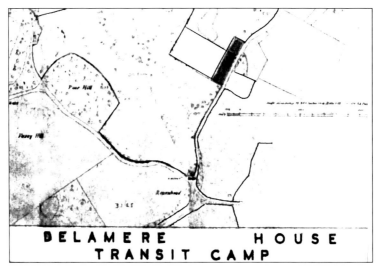

A plan of Delamere House Transit Camp, 1939. At this stage George Wilbraham retained upwards of forty acres of the Delamere House parkland.

arise in Britain in wartime. There were the bricklayers who asked for danger money to work during an air raid alert; there was the Garrison Engineer who could see poetry in the efficient mechanical workings of a sewage plant; and the American heavy tanks which churned up the newly-made camp roads."

As was customary, Singleton and the Army renamed the Delamere House Transit Camp as "Delamere Park Camp", whilst Oulton became "Oulton Park Camp". Neither the Wilbrahams, nor the Grey Egertons, had ever previously used "Park" in the titles of their family seats and yet, sixty years after the war, the word is instantly synonymous with both.

Laing huts, each to accommodate thirty men and an NCO, were erected by William Thornton, contractors of Liverpool, and a network of roads provided the basis for Delamere Park Camp. Nostalgic Americans later christened these roads from the New York grid system, Central Avenue, Fifth Avenue, Second Avenue etc., and established their headquarters and officers' mess around the foundations of Delamere House which, with the formal gardens and other land, was part of approximately forty additional acres requisitioned from George Wilbraham. It is said that much of the hardcore used in the construction of the roads and buildings came from blitzed houses in Liverpool.

The Americans began to arrive early in 1942, but not in significant numbers until the start of 1944 and the preparations for the invasion of Europe. The countryside around Mid Cheshire was soon swarming with "Yanks", notably at Delamere Park, Oulton Park, Marbury Park (Northwich), and Pettypool (Sandiway) which together accommodated in the region of 50,000 troops. Approximately 15,000 of these were at Delamere Park Camp, what the Americans knew as Camp Delamere, officially "Base 534 Cuddington".

"Donut Dugout" restaurants appeared in the district, huge stocks of military hardware were stored on the uncompleted stretch of the Hartford-Sandiway bypass, the local countryside became a training ground and the pubs and cinemas were awash with American GIs. As in the rest of Britain, the stories of their antics are legendary, but generally their friendliness and generosity endeared them to wary locals, inherently distrustful of all "foreigners". The White Barn, Cuddington, a favourite haunt of the American troops, always maintained strict

American barracks and water tower, looking west along what is now Denehurst Park Way.

segregation, as one villager recalls: "The Yanks were welcome in the best side, but they were definitely never allowed in the tap room; that was for locals only." The GI pranksters got their revenge by making off with a hefty four-legged table, literally from under the landlord's nose. It was later discovered at Camp Delamere and duly returned.

On another occasion, in 1944, the GIs were taking shooting practice in a quarry next to Wilbraham's Camomile Farm and when tired of stationary targets they turned their rifles on the neighbouring hens, a "turkey shoot" that bagged forty. Naturally, not best pleased, Farmer Stretch stormed up to the camp to confront the C.O. and for weeks afterwards food parcels, including such rarities as chocolate and oranges, were delivered to the farm! Elsewhere, one of the daughters of a Wilbraham cottager, in Crabtree Green, set up a "Comfort for the Boys" post, the "comfort" being personally administered in a tent pitched on a neighbouring field. The young woman was eventually hauled before the Quarter Sessions in Knutsford and sentenced to two weeks' imprisonment for damaging crops!

Understandably, since they were here for only a brief period, attempts to garner American memories of Camp Delamere have largely been unsuccessful, but some have been found, as follows:

Robert Lannan (368 Engineer GS Regiment): November 2, 1943 – Arrived Avonmouth; November 3 – Camp Delamere (training and building tent camps for those to come); April 16, 1944 – To Bedgellert for training; July 24 – Weymouth to board LSTs; July 26,27 – Landed at Utah Beach, Normandy.

Gene Harbener, 475th Military Police Escort Guard Company: November 3, 1944 – The 475 was transported to Camp Delamere, near Cuddington, Cheshire where it served as post MPs and did duty as town patrol in the city of Chester. November 13 – company moved to Spring Hill, near Bourton-on-the-Hill, above Moreton in Marsh, Gloucestershire.

History of the US 80th Division: July 4, 1944 – set sail aboard the Queen Mary, landing a few days later at Greenock, on the Firth of Clyde. The Division proceeded south to Northwich, England, via

One of the Camp Delamere Laing huts, erected to accommodate the Americans, thirty men and an NCO to each.

The water tower, looking east to Denehurst Park Way. The modern Paddock Walk houses are built on the site of the barrack huts in front of the open ground. The sycamore tree was one of many on the park tested by George Fortescue Wilbraham to establish if they were valuable Burr sycamores.

trains for additional training. Training included learning how to use waterproof equipment for the upcoming channel crossing. The Division crossed the English Channel in LSTs and Liberty Ships landing in Normandy on Utah Beach shortly after noon on August 2, 1944, D-Day + 57 and assembled near St. Jores, France. A few days later on August 8, 1944, the 80th was initiated into battle when it took over the Le Mans bridgehead in the XX Corps area. By the end of the war, May 7, 1945, the 80th Division had seen 277 days of combat. I t had captured 212,295 enemy soldiers. The 80th Division returned to the United States in January 1946, after spending time in Europe helping to restore and keep peace after the war.

Private George L.Vaughan: October 12, 1944 – Boarded Queen Mary for overseas crossing. Twenty thousand troops aboard. After five days at sea we landed in Scotland. Gee, it's beautiful here; the harbor is a wonderful sight. October 17 – Leaving ship at Glasgow harbor to board train for trip down through England. I noticed bomb damage was rather slight. October 18 – Arrived at Camp Delamere, in England. This was the worst place I had seen up to this time. The food was terrible and housing conditions for the troops were worse. We remained there for a week. Almost every night we used to go to a little town drinking, near the camp. It was a typical English town named Northwick (sic). We sat around in the pubs drinking that lousy English beer and singing songs. Little did we realize what lay ahead, or perhaps we might have drunk a little more beer, or sung a little louder. October 23 – Travelled by train to Southampton. It took us two days to cross; we had an escort of destroyers. We landed in Normandy on Omaha Beach. I saw at least 5,000 or 6,000 graves right on the beach.

Private Vaughan was later taken prisoner during a fierce battle in France in which seven of his "buddies", out of a squad of ten that had passed through Camp Delamere, were killed. At first the camp served as a staging post for a never-ending stream of troops who stayed only briefly, en route from Scotland to the South Coast, to await the invasion. The overwhelming majority of Americans who came to Camp Delamere and Mid Cheshire were not directly involved in the Normandy landings as they were held in reserve as part of General George S. Patton's US 3rd Army which, after D-Day, punched through the western side of the Cherbourg Peninsula, to close the Falaise pocket and then to be the main strike force into Germany.

General Patton's headquarters were at Peover Hall, near Knutsford, and he was a regular worshipper at Over Peover Parish Church where the American flag (Old Glory) which he presented, still hangs. Local evidence is strong that the Americans had a landing strip, on

General George Patton gave a rousing speech to troops of the American 3rd Army.

The last days of the Americans at Camp Delamere. Captain Musgrave (left) with Warrant Officer Wyatt Stone who met his English wife-to-be at a dance in Winsford. (Supplied by Ms J.Jones)

Wilbraham land at Crabtree Green, for senior officers arriving by light aircraft. Prior to D-Day, Patton is believed to have stayed at least one night at the Blue Cap, Sandiway, where he was joined by General Dwight D Eisenhower (later to become the 34th President of the United States) and General Omar Bradley. On that day, a grand parade took place at Camp Delamere as Patton, known to the media as "Blood and Guts", addressed his men with the same rousing speech he delivered at other 3rd Army camps in the area.

Patton's whereabouts was top secret, as he pointed out: "Don't forget, you don't know I'm here. No word of the fact is to be mentioned in any letters. The world is not supposed to know what the hell became of me. I'm not supposed to be commanding this Army. I'm not even supposed to be in England."

He concluded: "There is one great thing you men will all be able to say when you go home. You may thank God for it. Thank God, that at least, thirty years from now, when you are sitting around the fireside with your grandson on your knees, and he asks you what you did in the war, you won't have to cough and say, 'I shovelled shit in Louisiana'."

Almost overnight, in mid-June 1944, the American forces slipped out of

Camp Delamere to join the mass exodus towards the South coast and mainland Europe. Column upon column, singing as they went, marched through Pinfold Hollows and past the ancient mill of Cuddington to the railway station at Acton Bridge. The old village would never forget the "Yanks".

For months afterwards Camp Delamere continued as an American base, but instead of housing combat troops it became a depot, a holding point for thousands of tons of military supplies, shipped into Liverpool en route to the Continent. When the war came to an end and the last Americans left, the British returned to Delamere Park Camp in the form of a Royal Pioneer Corps' depot, transferred from Prestatyn, North Wales. The camp was large and almost empty and for a short period it was turned into a prison under the Pioneers who erected coiled barbed-wire entanglements around much of the perimeter fencing. These were not POWs, as local legend would sometimes have it, but the British Army's own "bad lads" who were awaiting trial, or who had been sentenced to twenty-eight days for their misdemeanors. This was in 1946 and a new occupation of Delamere Camp was about to commence in earnest.

Two American Fire Tender sheds were sited on Delamere Park Camp. This one, near to the old village settlement, was used for many years after the war as a farm building and is now a dwelling, "The Tank Shed", a name that has, misleadingly, come to be associated with military tanks. The other Fire Tender shed was demolished to allow for construction of the very last house to be built on Delamere Park, 1 Uplands.

Above: The present head of the Wilbraham family, Hugh Wilbraham, at Brook House (Bag Lane), in 1944, with his sisters Jane and Diana, and Lieutenant John Skinner, of the US Army.

Left: Hugh's father, Ralph Wilbraham was forty-five when he volunteered to rejoin the army in 1939. Taken prisoner, near to Rouen in 1940, he spent five years in captivity, latterly being held at a camp near to Cassel, in Germany. Here he was later joined by his brother-in-law, Captain J.H.Kershaw, of Onston Hall, a glider pilot wounded and captured at Arnhem. When the Allied armies crossed the Rhine, the German guards tried to evacuate the prisoners to the East, but after six days they were released by General Patton's spearhead troops.

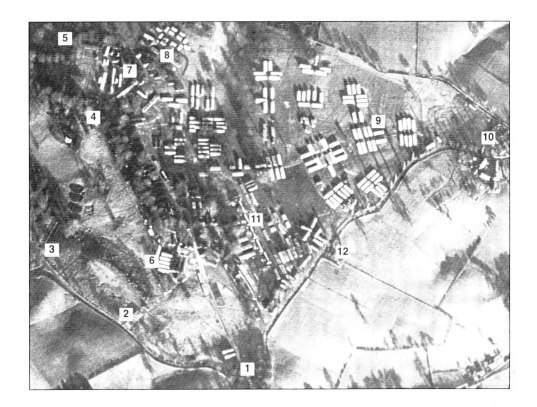

An RAF reconnaissance photograph (courtesy of English Heritage), of the 1946 Delamere Camp and the last vestiges of United States Army occupation.

1. Main Entrance to Central Avenue at South Lodge.

2. Fire Tender shed near to the modern Norley Road entrance.

3. Sewage Plant.

4. Gardener's Cottage.

5. Home Farm.

6. Mess Halls and Kitchens.

7. Headquarters Buildings with former Victorian walled gardens.

8. Officers' accommodation, on the bank overlooking what is now The Chines.

9. Barrack huts.

10. Fire Tender shed opposite to Poplar Farm.

11. Possibly the US Army stores/logistics area.

12. Gardens of demolished Park Lane cottages.

Delamere Camp

IT is almost impossible in the 21st century to imagine that amidst the former grandeur and modern affluence of Delamere Park, this was once the setting for one of the largest displaced persons' camps in the North West of England. The roots of "Delamere Camp", as it became known throughout the area, lay in war-ravaged Europe, thousands of miles away and long before Patton's United States 3rd Army invaded Mid Cheshire.

In 1939, the Soviet Union and Germany partitioned Poland and, in four mass deportations, an estimated 1.5 million Polish men, women and children, mainly from the east of the country, were expelled, thrust into cattle trucks at gunpoint and transported to remote labour camps, in Siberia and Kazakhstan. Stalin intended to strip Poland of its leading citizens so the country would be unable to form a democracy and, to this end, he ordered 10,000 Polish officers to be shot and buried in the Katyn forest. One of the few to escape the massacre, a single Russian soldier noticing his cross and allowing him to slip away, was a Polish chaplain, Father Antoni Manturzyk who was later to become the priest and a legend at Delamere Camp.

The tides of war shifted and when Hitler turned his might on the Soviet Union, the principle of a Polish army of POWs was agreed, under the command of General Wladyslaw Anders, and, begrudgingly, Stalin permitted the unarmed, emaciated prisoners to trek down to Persia (Iran) to join with the British. In his book "An Army In Exile", Anders wrote: "Anyone deprived of rations simply starved. It was with the greatest difficulty that I persuaded the Soviet authorities that including civilian women and children with the convoys was the only way to save them from starvation. Hundreds of thousands of Poles had already perished in transit and reserve centres."

A postcard commemorating the Battle of Monte Cassino with British Army and Polish 2nd Corps insignia. The White Eagle, the coat of arms of the Polish state, appears, with red crown, on many photographs from Delamere Camp. In Poland itself, the crown was removed during the years of Communist rule, to mark the country losing its independence as a free state.

The Polish army was eventually formed, trained and equipped in Tehran and sailed from Palestine to serve with the British 8th Army in Italy. The women and children were sent to India and North Africa, to see out the war in relative safety. By 1944, the Polish forces, numbering around 50,000, including Ukranians, Belarusans, Lithuanians, Latvians, suffered heavy losses in the Italian campaign, a fifth of their number falling during the assault on Monte Cassino which, after months of fighting and failure, was taken by the 2nd Polish Corps, commanded by General Anders. After the end of the war, divisions of the Polish Corps remained in Italy until 1946 when they were shipped from Naples to Liverpool, by which time, at the Yalta Conference, Britain and the United States had shamefully endorsed Poland becoming part of the Soviet sphere in post-war Europe. The bulk of Polish troops, angry and betrayed, would never again see their homeland, or live to witness its return to freedom.

To accommodate the Polish forces, the British government set up the Polish Resettlement Corps (PRC), an army-in-exile, under the auspices of the British Army and General Anders. All those, the majority, who wished to remain in the West were required to serve in the PRC for a minimum of two years in order to ensure residential qualification. PRC camps were established throughout the North West and North Wales, locally at Oulton Park and Delamere Park. Smaller camps were at Vale Royal and Pettypool and former Polish army officers, many freed from the infamous Colditz prison, were billeted at Blakemere

The South Lodge main entrance to the Polish Resettlement Corps' camp, in the late 1940s. When the camp's status was changed to accommodate displaced persons, the Polish signs and insignia were removed.

Hall, Sandiway. All came under Delamere Park Camp PRC Command and central to the structure were facilities provided by the Polish Medical Corps, based at the former 129th US Army Hospital, at Penley, near Wrexham.

In those early days of the PRC, four hundred former fighting troops were detailed to Delamere Park Camp, still partially occupied by a small unit of the British Pioneer Corps, congregated around the former US headquarters and the site of the old house. The Polish troops, commanded by Liaison Officer, Major Otto Sabritski, were housed in the area of modern Hollow Oak Lane and Cuddington Lane, previously used by the American Military Police.

The PRC carried out numerous duties on behalf of the British army, at home and abroad, until eventually, between 1947 and 1949, they were formally discharged. Consequently, some of the Mid Cheshire camps were beginning to empty, whereas at Delamere Camp, numbers started to rise as women and children, marooned in North Africa and India for the duration of the war, were brought to Britain to join their menfolk. Soon the Delamere Camp Laing huts were being taken over as family quarters by people who possessed little more than the clothes on their backs. Each family was allocated one-third of a barracks, partitioned with army blankets, and the Polish women turned these makeshift abodes into what one witness described as "little palaces", with lace

Three families to each barrack hut was the allocation when Delamere Camp was first occupied after the war by the Polish Resettlement Corps. The oak tree here is still standing, next to the tennis courts.

and embroidery to brighten up the drab walls, and gardens meticulously culti-vated with flowers and vegetables. To many of the former nomadic Eastern European troops, those who had endured unimaginable hardship and misery in the death camps of the Soviet Union, on their trek across Siberia and on the bat-tlefields such as Monte Cassino, these were the first homes they had known for over ten years. And so grew a proud, hardworking little community, undaunted by their poverty-stricken existence or their primitive conditions, without indi-vidual lavatories, baths or running water, and with only a central stove for heat-ing and an electric ring to cook upon.

A Polish committee ran the camp and the names of some of the American roads were changed to Sikorski Avenue and Second Chopin Avenue, and in one of the large surviving American mess huts, the men fashioned a church and prayed with Father Manturzyk, ever hopeful that, one day, Poland would be free.

In the years immediately after the war, when government and local authori-ties were struggling to get Britain back onto its feet, the Delamere "Polish"

Another view of the main entrance to the PRC Camp with Nissen huts and, in the distance, a brick water tank. The main sign, above the gate, "Delamere Park Camp" was almost certainly left by the British forces. On the white post, next to the lodge, is the Polish 2nd Corps' badge.

RAF aerial photograph (courtesy of English Heritage), dated 1950, showing Delamere Camp when occupied by the Polish Resettlement Corps and the British Pioneer Corps. It is clear that, by this time, many of the former US Army huts had been removed.

1. Main camp entrance at South Lodge.
2. Two large huts, possibly the US camp guard room, used by the Pioneer Corps as a reception area for incoming prisoners.
3. Central Avenue.
4. Polish Church, located in US Mess Hut alongside Central Avenue.
5. Former US officers' accommodation block occupied by Pioneer Corps.
6. Cuddington village entrance.
7. Second Chopin Avenue entrance, what is now Hollow Oak Lane.
8. Concentration of Laing huts occupied by the PRC.

Camp, like similar sites across the country, was left to itself, isolated, out of sight, out of mind. However, matters were to change dramatically in 1949/50 following the announcement of a national programme to relocate blitzed families to rural areas. At the same time, ICI began to advertise hundreds of new jobs as part of a large-scale expansion of its plants in Mid Cheshire and, as a consequence, Northwich Rural District Council embarked upon a programme of compulsory land purchase in the villages of Weaverham, Barnton, Leftwich and Cuddington & Sandiway, prime sites upon which to build over one thousand council houses for the deluge of newcomers, "imported workers" as they were termed, mainly from Liverpool.

The ICI jobs and the demand for housing were instant and Delamere Camp, then exclusively a Polish/Eastern European camp, was transferred to the Ministry of Housing & Local Government and officially reclassified as a Displaced Persons' Camp under the direct control of Northwich RDC and the National Assistance Board. Help was on the way for the Polish community, but it came at a price. Accommodation was to be made available on the camp for four hundred British families, bombed out of their homes, or awaiting housing allocation, and so, utilising Ministry of Housing aid, the local authority set about resurfacing the roads, removing surplus barrack huts and modernising the primitive living conditions. Two families instead of three were allocated to the huts, each with sitting room, two bedrooms, kitchen, running water, sanitation, electricity and stoves for heating and cooking.

The camp took on a new life although the Polish and British communities, with their different values, cultures and language, did little more than co-exist in an underlying climate of mistrust and misunderstanding. The newly-built council houses were prioritized in favour of the British, but those on Delamere Camp were, at first, largely ignored, as indicated in a letter to the local newspaper from "Hut Dwellers" who complained that only eight of their number had been allocated tenancies during 1950/1951. Eventually the situation improved and the British would often arrive and quickly depart the camp. Meanwhile, the Polish people got on with running the community in their own way.

The Roman Catholic church played a huge part in their daily lives; Easter,

An exercise in the fields, near to the former North Drive, for members of the Polish Resettlement Corps who had to serve under semi-military conditions for two years.

PRC soldier W.Pozniak (left) with Officers Arhamowicz and Abramczyk.

PRC troops circa 1948, alongside the site of the then recently demolished Park Lane cottages. The men may have just received their discharge papers.

Members of the Polish community outside the camp church which was housed in one of the former American mess halls. This was probably a Quonset hut, a semi-circular structure of corrugated steel, designed by the Americans as a much larger version of the British Nissen hut. One of the last wartime relics to survive on the camp it was not demolished until commencement of the housing development in the late 1960s.

The site of the Polish Church alongside modern Delamere Park Way West at its junction with The Cobbles.The Captain's Tree is in the background.

A summer's day outside the South Lodge, probably in the early 1950s after Delamere had been redesignated as a "Displaced Persons' Camp".

Lent and Christmas were special occasions and for Corpus Christi eight separate, decorated altars were erected around the camp, to be visited in procession led by the priest who conducted a short service at each. Later there was a doctor's surgery, nursery school, barber's shop, butcher's shop, laundry, chip shop, post office, mobile grocer's, cobbler's shop, cinema and clubhouse.

Many of the children were pupils at Sandiway County Primary School, or at St Werburghs, Chester, and all had to attend Saturday morning lessons on the camp, to learn the Polish language, culture and history. On all sides, the language barrier created enormous problems and, during the 1950s, some of the children, whose parents managed to scratch together their tuition fees, were sent to boarding schools run by Polish teachers, in Pitsford, near Leicester, and in Thetford.

Following discharge from the PRC, a number of Polish men journeyed to South Wales, to find employment in the coal and steel industries, whilst others emigrated to the United States and Canada, though most stayed and went to work at the ICI Winnington and Wallerscote plants. The great tragedy was that, due to language problems, the majority found only menial labouring jobs, in spite of the fact, in their own country, many had been well educated and were professionally qualified. They came to be known in their workplaces as "Ted the

The Roman Catholic Church and Father Manturzyk were at the heart of the Polish Camp community. The middle photograph shows the church interior. The procession is passing along Central Avenue.

Pole", "Joe the Pole", "Jan the Pole" etc, for as one ICI man put it, "It was the best way to remember them because their proper names often contained just about every letter in the alphabet". Life was equally difficult, and perhaps more harsh, for the women, many of whom went to work in clothing factories in Winsford, or at nearby Horner's Creamery. Others cleaned at the large houses, or found seasonal employment, backbreaking and poorly paid, on local farms, fruit-picking in Kelsall and potato-gathering in Cuddington. Throughout their years at Delamere Camp, the Polish people, and those of the other East European nationalities, were officially classed as identity card-carrying aliens and their credentials and their camp huts were subjected to annual scrutiny by the local police.

The first of the Mid Cheshire council houses were occupied as early as 1949 but it was to be many long years before the last Polish residents were to leave Delamere Camp and, when the time came, most were reluctant to do so. As late as 1960, and noting there still remained one-hundred families in occupation of the barrack huts, Northwich RDC minutes record a meeting between council officers and representatives of the "Polish Tenants Community", to plan the way forward:

"The Polish representatives stated that they had been very happy at Delamere Park and were worried at the break-up of their community. It was stressed that the council's decision could not be altered and that the park would have to close within approximately three years."

It was an unhelpful response as far as the Polish tenants were concerned and, almost in desperation, they pleaded with "Lord Wilbraham" to allow them to build their own houses on the camp site. George Wilbraham, determined to recover the site for far more profitable purposes, was having none of it. Other similar camps had long been emptied and returned to their original owners and, quite simply, he wanted the people out. He and his wife Bertha had done their duty for the war effort, the landed gentry at the big house supporting good causes and giving shelter to evacuees, but in the aftermath of hostilities George Wilbraham was once again encountering serious money problems and the sale of three long-standing estate properties (Ruloe House, Masseys Lodge and The

Mount) had only temporarily boosted his flagging coffers.

The winding-up of Delamere Camp was a laborious process controlled by Ministry of Housing & Local Government funding and, each month, Northwich RDC had to make formal application to remove the huts as they became vacant, on the grounds of "unfit for human habitation". One local authority report to the Ministry lists the following: 33 First Avenue, 15-19 Third Avenue, 34 Fifth Avenue, 3 Sixth Avenue, 9,19,44 Ninth Avenue, 24,6,10 Twelfth Avenue, 40 Thirteenth Avenue, 18,41,54 Central Avenue. Amidst all, there appears an example of bureaucratic intransigence concerning the 8th Northwich Scout Group who had purchased one of the derelict huts for the sum of £55, an amount which the scout leaders, supported by the council, considered excessive, especially as the building would otherwise have ended on a bonfire. The Ministry refused to budge, stating that the true figure should, in any case, have been £70.

Meanwhile, George Wilbraham had little choice but to wait, the Delamere House parkland's return being almost as far out of reach as it had been at the start of hostilities. In 1953 he wrote in the Wilbraham Diary:

Polish women from the camp employed by George and Bertha at Sweetbriar Hall. Left to right: Katarzyna Kolpas Szmigielska (housekeeper), Agnieszka Szulc (silver cleaner) and Zenia Szmigielska (cook). Their stylish outfits were courtesy of clothes parcels delivered to the camp from the United States.

A milk bottle, on a ledge outside the door, shows this hut occupied in the early 1960s. The huts all around have been demolished and only the concrete bases remain alongside a dirt-track. The tree, which still stands, and Cuddington Water Tower, in the distance, precisely pinpoint the site as modern Springfields.

> Now that the war is over, and the Labour government, with its excessive taxes, has departed, My dear wife and I find that we are unable to continue to live at Delamere Manor, also it is nearly impossible to obtain any servants to live in, so "Sweet Briar Hall" comes into existence, being built at Gallowsclough.

Increased taxes, failure to recover the Delamere House parkland and, probably, the loss of revenue from the Weaver Navigation, swallowed into nationalisation of the waterways, were clearly at the root of George Wilbraham deciding to sell Delamere Manor and downsize to Sweetbriar Hall which he had built, by Fred Whitehead (Northwich), in Gallowsclough Lane, and named after the 16th century Nantwich ancestral home of the Wilbrahams. Edward Graham-Wood, a keen polo player and member of the Cheshire and Cheshire Forest Hunts, purchased the Manor and subsequently the property passed through the ownerships of John Summers and Peter Gaskell to Gary Barlow, the pop musician of "Take That" fame. When George Wilbraham placed Delamere Manor on the market it was described as a "charming modern Georgian-style country residence" with three entertaining rooms, domestic offices, five principal bedrooms, one dressing room, three bathrooms and three maids' rooms. Also included were two modern cottages and a bungalow and fourteen acres, along with rough shooting rights over 2,000 acres.

In 1952, the year prior to George Wilbraham selling Delamere Manor, the family name became indirectly embroiled in one of the most intractable crimes of the 20th century, a murder mystery that has fired public imagination for over half a century. George Wilbraham's second cousin, Roger Wilbraham (1871-1951) and his wife Constance lived for most of their married life at Overdale (Oakmere), a house originally built by George Fortescue Wilbraham and occupied for many years by his younger brother,

"l'affaire Dominica": Ann Wilbraham who, as Lady Drummond, was murdered with her husband and daughter in France.

Henry, who was Roger's father. Here Roger and Constance raised a family, including a daughter, Ann Wilbraham, who went on to marry Jack Drummond, a professor of biochemistry and chief scientific adviser to the Ministry of Food during the war. His work earned him a knighthood and, in August 1952, Sir Jack and Lady Ann Drummond took their ten-year-old daughter, Elizabeth, on holiday to Provence. Near the village of Lurs, about seventy-five miles from Aix, they settled down to camp, but that night, by the banks of the River Durance, all three were shot and viciously clubbed to death.

Eighteen months later a 75-year-old peasant farmer, Gaston Dominica, who lived on a nearby smallholding, was convicted of the murders and sentenced to the guillotine. This was later commuted to life imprisonment and in 1960 he was freed by Charles de Gaulle. Since then, more than a dozen books and thousands of newspaper articles have been published about "l'affaire Dominica" and the general view now is that Sir Jack Drummond was a spy, caught up in a secret battle between East and West over each bloc's leading scientists. The assassins, it is claimed, were four men who travelled from Germany with a known record of carrying out "contract work" for a communist organisation in Frankfurt. On that fateful night, they tracked down the Drummonds to Lurs. The driver of the alleged assassin's car was subsequently arrested by German police on another matter and confessed to his involvement in the Drummond murders. Significantly, he admitted to having been shown by the others a wallet, foreign currency and an intricate gold ring taken from the bodies. The ring, he said, was ornately engraved and mounted with a square watch with bevelled edges, an almost precise description of that given to French lawyers at the time of the tragedy by Lady Drummond's mother, Constance Wilbraham!

Overdale, circa 1920. Erected by George Fortescue Wilbraham and occupied by his brother Henry and then his nephew, Roger.

RAF aerial photograph (courtesy of English Heritage), dated June 1951, showing the Displaced Persons' Camp. The changes, implemented by Northwich Rural Council, are evident when compared against the aerial photograph of the camp in 1947. Many of the original huts have been demolished and only the bases remain.

1.   Main camp entrance at South Lodge.
2.   Allotments.
3.   Central Avenue.
4.   Polish Church. The other large huts alongside were
        demolished shortly after this photograph.
5.   Norley Road Fire Tender Sheds.
6.   Keepers Cottage.
7.   Sewage Plant.
8.   Hunt's Hill Wood.
9.   Woods Lane.
10.   Home Farm.
11.   General "British" area.
12.   Bases of former US headquarters building.
13.   Scout Hall, formerly Polish Laundry.
14.   Polish "school"/cinema.
15   Ninth Avenue.
16.   Barber's shop.
17.   Doctor's surgery.
18.   Camp Water Tower.
19.   Second Chopin Avenue, site of former US stores/logistics area.
20.   Polish shop.
21.   Sikorski Avenue.
22.   Bases of demolished huts.
23.   Park Lane.

Top left: The Polish war hero General Anders during a visit to Delamere Camp. Top right: Members of Franciszek Janik's family who lived on Second Avenue. Bottom left: Bozena Szymanska and Halina Szulc whose fathers were members of the Polish Camp Band. Halina's father, like others on the camp, had been in the Polish Resistance. Bottom right: Father Manturzyk with Delamere Camp Brownies in the 1950s.

With the White Eagle emblem of Poland in the background, a Christmas party and traditional celebrations for the children.

The photographs on these two pages emphasise the importance that the Roman Catholic religion had on everyday life. When the camp closed, a Polish Church committee purchased a large house adjacent to the Railway Arches, in London Road, Northwich, and here they built a new church and hall, still the focal point of the scattered Polish community in Mid Cheshire. Much of the finance for the project came from the people of Delamere Camp.

Outside the church, with the Captain's Tree and Cuddington Water Tower in the distance.

This view, from the South Lodge end of Central Avenue, shows Polish allotments and, beyond, a row of huts which were accessed via a dirt track midway between Central Avenue and Second Chopin Avenue.

These prefabricated huts with electrical substation and boiler house stood approximately on the site of the present Delamere Park Way West substation.

On Second Chopin Avenue, a procession of girls in Polish traditional dress passes by more of the prefabricated concrete huts.

The majority of Delamere Camp residents took a great pride in their surroundings and their families. The lady to the left, in her garden, is a Polish housewife. To the right is the Pozniak family in the mid-1950s, outside 19 Second Chopin Avenue.

George and Margaret Marsh, early occupants of the "British" huts which were located near to the site of Delamere House. The Marsh's son, Bernard, served for many years as clerk to Cuddington & Sandiway Parish Council. The prefabricated huts in the background were erected as accommodation for American officers.

A procession at Delamere Camp in the 1950s. Park Lane is to the left and in the distance is South Lodge. The procession is passing by the Polish allotments upon which stands one of the last Nissen huts. The houses of Threeways are now here.

Delamere Park, the Wilbraham legacy

APPROACHING seventy and, perhaps, a hostage to fortune, George Wilbraham gambled heavily on the development potential of the Delamere House parkland, still years away from government de-requisitioning and the due process of formal planning approval. He had lost control of the land at the outbreak of war and by 1960 the repercussions lingered on, interminably. With his solicitor in tow, as members of the Polish community remember, he prowled the camp in search of squatters who, quick to occupy any empty barracks awaiting demolition, would further compound his problems.

Unfortunately for the Captain, the wheels of bureaucracy turn slowly and

The last "resident" of the old camp was Jan Wierzbicki, better known as "Jan the Hermit". He had taken to living rough on the derelict site in the 1960s and for over twenty years lived in his battered caravan in the triangle of rhododendrons at the junction of Cuddington Lane and Norley Road.

WILBRAHAMS OF DELAMERE

1. George Wilbraham
Son (1741-1813) of Roger Wilbraham and Mary Hunt, of Townsend House, Nantwich. Built Delamere Lodge. Sheriff of Cheshire, MP for Bodmin (1789-90), Founder member of the Tarporley Hunt Club (1762). Married (1774) Maria Harvey, daughter of William & Emma Harvey, of Rolls Park, Chigwell, Essex. Issue: Maria, Emma, Roger (died 1784), George, William, Elizabeth, Louisa, Anna.

2. George Wilbraham
Son (1779-1852) of George Wilbraham, born Hefferston Grange, Weaverham, Cheshire. MP for Stockbridge, Hants, Chester and Cheshire (1826-1842), Sheriff of Cheshire (1844). Married (1814) Lady Anne Fortescue (1788-1864), daughter of Hugh, Viscount Ebrington, 1st Earl Fortescue, of Filleigh, Devon. Issue: George Fortescue, Roger William, Thomas Edward, Henry, Hugh.

3. George Fortescue Wilbraham
Son (1815-1885) of George Wilbraham, born Delamere Lodge. Home Circuit barrister, Sheriff of Cheshire. Died unmarried without issue

4. Roger Wilbraham
Brother (1817-1897) of George Fortescue Wilbraham, born Delamere Lodge. Parliamentary Secretary to the Rt. Hon. William Gladstone. Married (1850) Louisa Gosling (1831-1901), daughter of Robert Gosling, of Botley's Park, Surrey. Issue: Arthur George (died 1886), Hugh Edward, Herbert Vere, Henry Dudley, Frederick William, William Robartes, Alice Mary, Beatrice Augusta, Ada Louisa.

5. Hugh Edward Wilbraham
Son (1858-1930) of Roger Wilbraham, born Godlaming, Surrey. Alderman of Cheshire, Justice of the Peace, MBE for Public Service. Married (1887) Lilla Jane Coney (1863-1952), daughter of Rev. Thomas Coney, of Braywick, Berkshire. Issue: George Hugh de Vernon, Ralph Venables, Vera May, Rhoda Joan, Barbara Francesca.

6. George Hugh de Vernon Wilbraham
Son (1890-1962) of Hugh Edward Wilbraham, born Masseys Lodge, Oakmere, Cheshire. Demolished Delamere House, 1939. Married 1 (1919) Kathleen Mary Neilson, daughter of Henry Cottingham Neilson, of Plovers Moss, Oakmere, Cheshire; 2 (1937) Mary Roberta Bullock (1909-1996) daughter of William John Bullock, of Malton, Yorkshire. Died without issue.

7. Hugh Dudley Wilbraham
Nephew (1929 -) of George Hugh de Vernon Wilbraham, born Brook House, Cuddington, Cheshire. Married (1957) Laura Jane McCorquodale, daughter of George McCorquodale. Issue: Ian Hugh (1958 -), Philip George (1960 -), James Christopher (1964 -), Fiona Laura Mary (1967 -)

the Ministry of Housing and Northwich Rural Council would not be rushed; besides, the building of council houses in the district had slowed to a trickle, largely due to a significant contraction in demand from ICI. Few of the remaining Polish families were likely be allocated new council houses and vacant tenancies were infrequent.

The only immediate course left to George Wilbraham was to open negotiations with the government in anticipation of the final return of the former parkland. The War Department had paid £60 an acre and this was to be the sum at which it would be offered to him as the original owner, unless military occupation could be shown to have seriously damaged the land. It was a sop, of course, for there were few military sites that had not been severely scarred. All George had to do was prove it and the land would be his without any outlay whatsoever. To meet the necessary criteria, the Northwich photographer, Lawrence Sands, was engaged to record the sorry state of the camp with its former military roads and hundreds of concrete bases upon which the barrack huts had stood. The deal was done in principle, leaving George Wilbraham in a position to borrow from his bank against Ministry of Housing & Local Government assurances that

The last days of South Lodge, in April 1969. Its remains lie beneath the bank alongside the Wilbraham Gate.

Listed building status was placed on the former American Fire Tender shed on the edge of Cuddington old village. The property was purchased in 2003 and has since been converted into a family home, "The Tank Shed", by its owners, Mike Parker and Debra Dexter.

planning approval would be granted to develop the site. He had waited for over twenty years and then, ironically, did not see it come to pass.

On January 16, 1962, George Hugh de Vernon Wilbraham, who will forever be remembered as the man who demolished Delamere House, died at Sweetbriar Hall, the future of the Wilbraham Estate and the Delamere House parkland thrown into turmoil. The Cheshire Life magazine described Captain Wilbraham as "one of the county's most colourful personalities, an elder statesman of the Tarporley Hunt Club and a senior magistrate".

George's executors were his wife Bertha and his solicitor, Rae Cullimore, of Birch Cullimore, Chester, who together had the unenviable task of unravelling and reconciling what must have been a complicated set of affairs. Indeed, by the time probate was granted, in May 1962, almost half of George's personal estate had been wiped out, primarily, one supposes, in settling the bank debt, and death duty was temporarily in abeyance. By the terms of his will, George Wilbraham's estate was to remain in trust for the benefit of his wife and, after her death, pass to his nephew, Ralph Wilbraham's son, Hugh Dudley Wilbraham.

Finally, around the end of 1963, the last of the Polish families left the camp and the once stately parkland was returned to George Wilbraham's executors who immediately sought outline planning permission for housing. The majority of residents of Cuddington & Sandiway and Norley were opposed to a development they considered a threat to the district's rural tranquility, a traffic-generating village within a village, four hundred houses where once there had been one. It became an emotive issue in some quarters and Northwich Rural District Council utilised a planning regulations technicality to refer the decision directly to the Ministry of Housing & Local Government, a manoeuvre which patently endorses the view that the site was returned with a promise. To have reinstated the camp site to its "agricultural" classification of the 1930s was totally unrealistic and, consequently, local opposition was always destined to fail at a charade of public inquiry, in May 1964.

Two months later, Sir Keith Joseph, the Minister of Housing & Local Government, duly ruled in favour of the development. Noting demand for larger types of houses for those in executive and managerial positions, the accompanying report stated: "The Minister accepts that the restoration of this land to agriculture or forestry would be uneconomic and that it could be appropriately used for housing and ancillary development of a high standard. Consideration should be given to the desirability of reserving land for communal facilities proportionate to the size of the estate."

George Wilbraham's executors wasted little time in disposing of their valuable asset and in the following March, 1965,

they formally sold the Delamere House parkland, approximately ninety-six acres, to Salvesen Properties (Development) Limited, part of the Christian Salvensen Group. During the following four years, the camp lay derelict, a wilderness of tangled brambles, weeds and rabbits. The tar-macadamed roads became a haven for local youngsters learning the rudiments of driving and only the two Tank Shed buildings, the American mess hall and the South Lodge remained, the latter stripped of its lead and slates long before demolition.

At the beginning of 1970, the local authority approved the first phase of what became known as the Delamere Park development, to be laid out at 4.8 houses per acre, six bed-spaces per house, as specified in Sir Keith Joseph's rec-

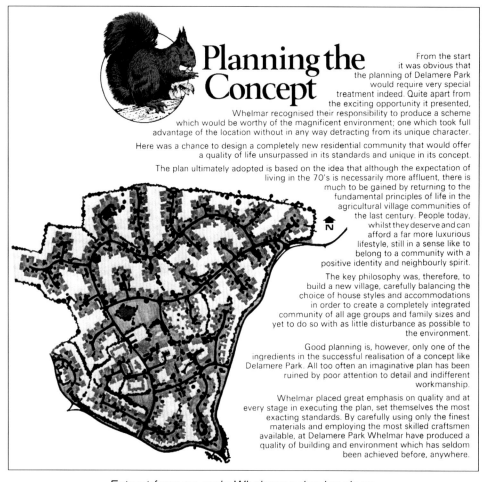

Planning the Concept

From the start it was obvious that the planning of Delamere Park would require very special treatment indeed. Quite apart from the exciting opportunity it presented, Whelmar recognised their responsibility to produce a scheme which would be worthy of the magnificent environment; one which took full advantage of the location without in any way detracting from its unique character.

Here was a chance to design a completely new residential community that would offer a quality of life unsurpassed in its standards and unique in its concept.

The plan ultimately adopted is based on the idea that although the expectation of living in the 70's is necessarily more affluent, there is much to be gained by returning to the fundamental principles of life in the agricultural village communities of the last century. People today, whilst they deserve and can afford a far more luxurious lifestyle, still in a sense like to belong to a community with a positive identity and neighbourly spirit.

The key philosophy was, therefore, to build a new village, carefully balancing the choice of house styles and accommodations in order to create a completely integrated community of all age groups and family sizes and yet to do so with as little disturbance as possible to the environment.

Good planning is, however, only one of the ingredients in the successful realisation of a concept like Delamere Park. All too often an imaginative plan has been ruined by poor attention to detail and indifferent workmanship.

Whelmar placed great emphasis on quality and at every stage in executing the plan, set themselves the most exacting standards. By carefully using only the finest materials and employing the most skilled craftsmen available, at Delamere Park Whelmar have produced a quality of building and environment which has seldom been achieved before, anywhere.

Extract from an early Whelmar sales brochure.

ommendations. Somewhere along the way, the "4.8 houses per acre" condition was reduced to just over "4 houses per acre" as Whelmar Limited, a subsidiary of Christian Salvesen Properties, commenced the construction programme which was estimated to continue for upwards of five years.

Delamere Park was the dream of Tom Baron, a director of Whelmar Limited, who had visited stand-alone, self-managed villages in the United States, a concept he was certain would be successful in Britain. Tom Baron took personal control of the development and, by October, 1971, the first house was occupied, in Dingle Way. Others quickly followed and Cuddington Parish Council, consulted on the choice of names for the various roads, favoured Downham Parkway, Halton View and Wilbraham Drive, none of which materialised.

In those early days, Tom Baron's dream included the building of a primary school, shops and a clubhouse and these were expressly set out in a master plan included within an agreement between Cheshire County Council and Whelmar Limited. The shops and the school subsequently became another emotive issue locally and by the time of the final completion of Delamere Park, at the end of the 1970s, both had been dropped from the development. The clubhouse went ahead and within it, marking his immense input into the development of the park, was the Tom Baron Room. His vision of self-management by the residents, termed "plot holders", was his most enduring legacy. Through a covenant within their deeds, the plot holders pay an annual fee (initially £20) and, from within their midst, appoint trustees as Directors of Delamere Park Management Committee, a body legally responsible for the maintenance and administration of the clubhouse and the amenity land on the park. It is worthy of note that Tom Baron and Whelmar Limited also developed similar Delamere Park-style villages in Warrington and Runcorn, neither of which has continued to be self-managed and the amenities are now maintained by their local authorities.

The National House Building Council voted Delamere Park as the North West's Best Development of the 1970s and, reporting on the accolade, the Northwich Guardian commented:

"Delamere Park has been something of an experiment for Whelmar, for the

The Wilbraham name is irrevocably interwoven into the fabric of the district and with upwards of one thousand acres, five farms and numerous cottages, it was fitting that Hugh Wilbraham, the head of the family and great, great, great, grandson of the founder of Delamere Lodge, should have been invited to formally open Delamere Park's Wilbraham Millennium Gate, on the site of the old South Lodge entrance. He is photographed with the project manager Alf Brooks (centre) and David Coxhead (left).

The Wilbraham family at the Gate-opening ceremony. Hugh Wilbraham is at the rear with his three sons, Ian, Philip and James.

once beautiful parkland had degenerated by the time the firm acquired it, into, in their own words, an almost impenetrable thicket. The village atmosphere is something the developers aimed for from the start. They did not set out to build a housing estate, but create a village, a rural community with a life of its own."

Delamere Park continues to thrive, as strong and attractive a community development as ever Tom Baron could have wished. The well-voiced epithet of "Oh, you live on the camp?" has disappeared with the passage of time from local lips and only one serious setback has marred the past thirty years. It occurred in March 2004 when the clubhouse, the focal point of the community, was destroyed by fire. As a consequence many difficulties were overcome and, true to the pledge of the majority of residents, a new clubhouse was opened two years later, principally due to the sterling efforts of Tim Winder, the then chairman of the Delamere Park Management Committee, and fellow directors, David Whitby and Graham Simpson, ably assisted by retired architect and Park Manager, Brian Elton.

The clubhouse once more contributes to the uniqueness of Delamere Park with its astonishing history of centuries... hidden, but not forgotten!

From the Northwich Guardian, March 17, 2004.

Then and now! The mature chestnut tree, featured in the top photograph of Delamere House from the 1920s, still stands in front of The Burrows, off Denehurst Park Way. The roads onto The Burrows and onto Badgers Sett almost precisely follow the line of the South Drive which swept towards the ornate gate and the main entrance to Delamere House.

Left: Modern Westrees along what would have been Delamere House's great central corridor, through the West Wing to the Conservatory and Walled Garden. Right: Number 1 Dingle Way, the home of the Holsteads since 1971, was the first house to be occupied on the Delamere Park development.

Left: The line of the South Drive looking along Three Ways towards Cuddington Water Tower. This is the modern view of the procession photograph on Page 160. Right: Number 1 Uplands, the last property to be built on Delamere Park, on the site of the Norley Road Fire Tender shed.

The modern Delamere Park road layout, with Norley Road and Woods Lane, over-laid onto the 1946 aerial photograph of Delamere Camp. The clubhouse is coloured orange. Yellow marks the site of Delamere House, the 200 square-feet conservatory and the coachhouse. The large green area alongside defines the Victorian walled gardens. In the centre of the plan, in blue, is the ornamental lake. The footpath from Cuddington village, around the eastern perimeter of the park, is shown in brown. (Plan by Norman Shelley)

Left: Delamere Park Way West photographed from its junction with The Spinney. The car is passing through the location of the portico entrance to Delamere House. Right: The Sycamore tree here, on the corner of Badgers Sett, appears on several camp photographs, notably on Page 130. The playingfield has always been open space.

Left: The Coppice, looking west. The Walled Garden was located to the right whilst further along, to the left, was the Arboretum. Several Sequoias and a giant Cedar survive here. Right: Delamere Park Way West looking towards the north and the approximate location of the girls on horseback, featured on Page 92.

Appendix

(1) The aquifer formed by the final glaciations has been critical to the ancient settlement of Cuddington. An enclosed sea, near to the Equator, deposited vast quantities of sand, its base compacted into sandstone. Tectonic plate movement carried the sea northwards, depositing the sand and salt as it evaporated. When this collided with the Cambrian mountains of the Atlantic, the plate buckled to form the Mid Cheshire sandstone ridge and here it deposited deep sand to form the Cheshire plain. Successive glaciers moved across Cheshire and the southern movement of the final one halted to form the Beeston Terminal Moraine. As this receded north-westwards it deposited, behind the Mid Cheshire ridge, a layer of Boulder Clay (crushed rock), 1-5 metres in thickness, laden with granite cobbles, many broken by the weight of ice.

Summer melts caused vast rivers to flow eastwards across the plain and through the Mouldsworth gap in the Mid Cheshire Ridge, so gouging the Kingsley-Norley-Cuddington Ridge. Minor advances and recessions of the c.800ft glacier, especially in the Weaverham area, blocked the eastwards flowing rivers, so creating a sea with the Cuddington Ridge as its southern edge. When this sea eventually overflowed, vast rivers rushed southwards through weak points in the clay-capped ridge and formed what are now the valleys of Cuddington Brook and Small Brook. The southward rivers flowed as far as Middlewich and Crewe and, as they diminished, they laid down the "Crabtree Green" sand.

On the Cuddington Ridge, the clay-capped, steep-sided plateau and its valleys were laden with ice. As this melted it caused the clay cap to sink, forming, over the whole of the plateau, a saucer-shaped aquifer with an elevated springline. Rich vegetative soil eventually capped the aquifer to form moist, fertile agricultural land upon which shallow wells, for drinking water, could be dug anywhere, so combining to make the plateau ideal for settlement.

(2) The Fee, or estate, of Kingsley, with twelve manors, was within the Forest of Mara & Mondrem (Delamere) and designated from the time of Hugh Lupus, Earl of Chester, as King's land, held on behalf of the Crown by Ranulph de Kingsley, the first Master Forester. The Fee was later sub-divided amongst four daughters of the de Kingsleys, each holding a quarter share. These shares descended through marriage and various sub-divisions so that by the time of the 1767 Bryn Common Enclosure, Richard Smith-Barry, John Arderne and Francis Wells claimed, dubiously in the opinion of the authors, to be "lords of the soil" of Cuddington.

(3) Joan de Kingsley, one of the daughters of the de Kingsley family, married Henry Done who became the Master Forester and several generations of Dones lived at Crowton Hall. Joan de Kingsley and her three sisters each held a quarter share in the Manor of Crowton. Joan's share descended through the Ireland family (Lancashire) and the Hatton family to the Arderne family. The Ardernes subsequently acquired two of the other quarter shares. The fourth share was vested in the Gerrard family and descended to Ralph Leycester, then being purchased by George Fortescue Wilbraham.

Index

This book represents only part of the research notes, photographs and documentation gathered by David Coxhead. He intends to eventually deposit his collection in the public archives.